M000220511

The F-14 Tomcat Story

The F-14 Tomcat Story

Tony Holmes

The
HISTORY
Press

Also in this series:

The Concorde Story

The Spitfire Story

The Vulcan Story

The Red Arrows Story

The Harrier Story

The Dam Busters Story

The Hurricane Story

The Lifeboat Story

The Tornado Story

The Hercules Story

Published in the United Kingdom in 2009 by
The History Press
The Mill · Brimscombe Port · Stroud · Gloucestershire · GL5 2QG

Copyright © Tony Holmes, 2009

British Library Cataloguing in Publication Data
A catalogue record for this book is available from the British
Library.

Hardback ISBN 978-0-7524-4985-2

Typesetting and origination by The History Press
Printed in Italy by L.E.G.O. S.p.A.

Half title page: *F-14As from VF-114 'Aardvarks'
and VF-213 'Black Lions' crowd the flightdeck of
USS* Enterprise *(CVN-65) between missions in the
Indian Ocean in August 1984. The wings of these
aircraft are locked in the 75° oversweep position
that was the norm for Tomcats when chained down
to a carrier deck. (US Navy via Peter Mersky)*

Title page: *Naval Aviators from VF-31 'Tomcatters'
practise their mirror formation manoeuvre
for the benefit of the camera during the unit's
Mediterranean/Indian Ocean cruise embarked in
USS* John F Kennedy *(CV-67) in early 1982. Both
F-14As are armed with live AIM-9M and AIM-7M
air-to-air missiles. (US Navy via Peter Mersky)*

CONTENTS

VF-213's F-14D 'Black Lion 210' formates with an
S-3B from VS-24 during routine cyclic operations over
the Atlantic from USS Theodore Roosevelt (CVN-71)
on 12 September 2005. The Tomcat has a LANTIRN
targeting pod attached to its starboard wing glove
pylon. (Lt Scott Timmester)

ACKNOWLEDGEMENTS

Two F-14A crews from VF-11 'Red Rippers' close up with their formation leader so that the Radar Intercept Officer (RIO) can take an 'I love me' shot for his album during CV-67's epic 1983-84 war cruise to the Mediterranean. (US Navy via Peter Mersky)

Over the past 20 years, I have written several books and countless magazine articles on the F-14 Tomcat, the squadrons that have been equipped with it and the Naval Aviators that have flown it. I grew up with the aircraft, as US Navy carrier battle groups would routinely visit my hometown of Fremantle, Western Australia, for spells of 'R&R' during their Indian Ocean and Pacific cruises in the 1980s. I am therefore very familiar with the Tomcat story!

As always when producing a volume such as this one, I call upon my regular contacts for photographs to help illustrate the colourful career of a naval aviation icon. Such a request usually opens up the floodgates, and it has been a real job to pare my selection down from the hundreds of images supplied to the 130 seen in this book. I would therefore like to thank Peter Mersky, Henk van der Lugt, Dave Brown, Richard Cooper, Tom Cooper, Angelo Romano, Bill Barto and Doug Siegfried at the Tailhook Association for their efforts on my behalf.

Tony Holmes

Few aircraft of the Cold War era have attained such cult status and adoration amongst those that flew it, wanted to fly it or kept it flying as the mighty Grumman F-14 Tomcat. As big, bold and brash as the *Top Gun* film in which it played the starring role in 1986, the US Navy's ultimate fleet fighter epitomised what naval aviation was all about throughout its three decades of service with its primary operator.

The Tomcat was the final creation of the Grumman Aircraft Corporation, which had been churning out fighters for the US Navy from its Bethpage, New York, plant since the 1930s. Wildcats, Hellcats, Tigercats, Panthers, Cougars and Tigers all darkened the flightdecks of aircraft carriers from World War II through to the Cold War. Like the various cats that these machines were named after, all Grumman aircraft had a reputation for being effective fighters that proved their durability in combat.

As the ultimate product of the Grumman 'Iron Works', the F-14 would inherit all the qualities of its feline forebears. Like them, it would marry good performance with immense strength – a necessity if the aircraft was to withstand the violence of operations from a pitching carrier deck at sea. The Tomcat also possessed handling

◄

Grumman's fleet fighter of the 1970s flies in formation with the 'Iron Works" product that defended US Navy carriers just three decades earlier. The FM-2 Wildcat had a maximum speed of 320 mph and weighed 7952 lbs when fuelled up and fully armed. The F-14A could attain 1553 mph in afterburner and tipped the scales at 74,349 lbs. (Grumman History Center via Tailhook)

qualities that made it more than a match for many of its opponents.

The F-14 was a big fighter in every sense of the word, tipping the scales at 74,349 lbs (33,724 kg) when fully loaded – Grumman's first fleet fighter, the biplane FF-1 of 1933, weighed in at just 4,828 lbs (2,190 kg)! Of the F-14's Cold War contemporaries, only the MiG-25 'Foxbat' was heavier, and pilots flying the Soviet interceptor had the luxury of operating them from vast runways in the USSR. When it comes to the unique environment of 'blue water ops', the Tomcat remains the largest fighter to have been sent to sea.

As this modest volume will hopefully illustrate, the size of the F-14 meant that it could be adapted to perform other roles aside from that for which it was originally built – fleet defence against missile-equipped Soviet bombers. With the thawing of the Cold War in the late 1980s, the Tomcat community was faced with a stark choice. Turn the aircraft into a multi-role strike-fighter platform such as its great rival, the F/A-18 Hornet, or stick steadfastly to the fighter mission and face almost certain extinction. The reality of this situation was brought home to Naval Aviators flying the F-14 during Operation *Desert Storm* in 1991. Whilst supporting the campaign to liberate Kuwait from Iraqi occupation, some 99 Tomcats embarked in five aircraft carriers logging more than 4,000 sorties as they performed combat air patrols, fighter escort missions for strike aircraft and aerial reconnaissance. However, the aircraft was usurped in its primary mission of air-to-air combat by the US Air Force's F-15C Eagle, which claimed 34 aerial victories to the F-14's one.

Lessons were quickly learned from *Desert Storm* to the extent that just weeks after the conflict had ended, Grumman's Field Service Department journal *Tomcat News* proclaimed, 'We should take heed of the writing on the wall and continue to press forward into the world of mud-moving!' As a Naval Aviator in the fighter community at Naval Air Stations Miramar or Oceana in the 1970s and 1980s, expressing such sentiments would have been viewed as sacrilegious. However, by 1992 the only way the Tomcat was going to keep its place on a carrier flightdeck was if it could drop bombs. Thanks to the aircraft's awesome load-carrying capacity, legendary long range and the advent of a bolt-on targeting sensor pod for precision bombing, the Tomcat evolved into the 'Bombcat', and it went on to play a pivotal role in the US military's 'War on Terror' from 2001 through to its retirement in 2006.

By then the F-14 was far from being in the flush of youth. Nevertheless, its

Four 2000-lb Mk 84 'iron' bombs are released by an F-14A from VF-51 over the Bravo 20 range at NAS Fallon, Nevada, during CVW-15's air wing work-ups in January 1994. (Cdr Tom Twomey)

➤

The end of the road for the mighty Tomcat. These F-14B/Ds are seen in storage with the 309th Aerospace Maintenance and Regeneration Group (AMARG) at Davis-Monthan Air Force Base, in Arizona. The last of these aircraft arrived at this site in September 2006, and since then a large number of retired Tomcats have been scrapped. (Richard Cooper)

'Although I am sure that I will love flying the Super Hornet, there was simply nothing bad about the Tomcat from a pilot's perspective. The F-14 was, and still is, simply a great aeroplane.'
Enough said!

contribution in Operations *Enduring Freedom* (2001-02) and *Iraqi Freedom* (2003-06) meant that the aircraft approached phasing out with its claws well and truly bared. Such was the feeling that the jet evoked amongst those that flew it, Cdr Curt Seth, commanding officer of the US Navy's last fighter squadron, made the comment above when asked how the F-14 compared with his new, considerably more modern, F/A-18E Super Hornet on the eve of his unit's transition to the latter type.

Grumman originally designed the F-14 Tomcat to perform one mission, and one mission only – fleet defence. The US Navy's need for a long-endurance aircraft that was capable of launching several high-speed long-range air-to-air missiles came about thanks to the improvement of Soviet missile technology in the late 1950s. Long-range cruise missiles launched from high-speed bombers at a stand-off distance of as much as 200 nautical miles posed the greatest threat to the 'jewel' in the US Navy's surface fleet 'crown', the carrier battle group.

By the early 1960s, Tupolev was churning out Tu-16, Tu-22 and Tu-95 bombers, all armed with Kh-series cruise missiles, at an alarming rate. The US Navy's F-4 Phantom II and F-8 Crusader, although both out-standing fighters against comparable Communist types such as the MiG-17 and MiG-21, lacked the radar performance and weaponry to adequately deal with Soviet bombers armed with cruise missiles. In order to defeat this ever-growing threat, a new type of interceptor was required. The US Navy needed a carrier-capable aircraft fitted with an incredibly powerful radar that could detect the bombers before they got to within launching range of the fleet.

The interceptor's weapon system would be crucial to its effectiveness in this role, and the missile chosen, in 1958, was the Bendix XAAM-M-10 Eagle. Like the bombers it would be hunting, the Eagle was a big missile. Appreciably larger than the much shorter-ranged air-to-air weapons carried by US Navy fighters at the time, the XAAM-M-10 was 16 ft (4.9 m) long and weighed 1,284 lbs (852 kg).

Did you know?
Grumman designers examined several configurations of swing- or fixed wings, single- or twin-fins and podded or submerged engines before settling on the then single-finned Model 303E.

This heavily modified NA-3A Skywarrior was used by the Hughes Aircraft Company during the 1960s as a flying testbed for the Phoenix Airborne Missile Control System (AMCS). It is seen here test firing a development AIM-54 over the Pacific Missile Range in 1967, shadowed by an F-9 Cougar chase aeroplane. The aircraft was fitted with an F-111B radome to house the AMCS antenna, radar and infrared subsystems. (Mike Glenn)

By comparison, American fleet fighters at that time were armed with 155-lb (70 kg) AIM-9B Sidewinder and/or 452-lb (205 kg) AIM-7E Sparrow missiles. The former had a range of two miles (3.2 km) and the latter 28 miles (44 km). The AAM-N-10, however, was designed to intercept targets some 127 miles (204 km) away.

Development of the Eagle was eventually taken on by Hughes Aircraft from 1960, and the company incorporated numerous aspects of the missile into its AIM-54 Phoenix (initially designated the AAM-N-11). This weapon emerged in the early 1960s as the most sophisticated, and most costly, air-to-air missile in the world. At the same time the company developed the AN/AWG-9 advanced fire control system to help detect targets for the Phoenix. Starting out life as the APN-122(V), the AWG-9 would have a track-while-scan capability that would allow it simultaneously to track 24 targets and attack six of them. And the latter – cruise missile-toting Soviet bombers – would be engaged at extreme range. Like the AIM-54, the AWG-9 was a weighty system, boasting the largest circular aerial of planar type radar antenna ever carried by a fighter. It also had stunning performance figures, with a look-down target acquisition capability out to 150 miles (241 km).

The aircraft that the US Navy hoped would defend the fleet with XAAM-M-10s guided by the pulse Doppler AN/AWG-9 radar was the Douglas F6D-1 Missileer. Boasting an unswept, shoulder-mounted, wing and non-afterburning engines that gave it a top speed of just Mach 0.8, the Missileer was the complete antithesis of the fast and highly agile F-14 Tomcat. The F6D-1 would have been able to carry out the anti-bomber role thanks to its war load of up to eight Eagle missiles, but it lacked any chance of defending itself in aerial combat against agile MiG fighters.

With the XAAM-M-10 suffering ongoing development problems, the Missileer was abandoned in December 1960. However, the AN/AWG-9 remained a viable project, with the Eagle being reborn as the AAM-N-11 Phoenix.

In 1961, in an effort to cut costs by avoiding duplication in the procurement of weapons systems, new Defense Secretary Robert S McNamara encouraged the development of a common USAF/US Navy fighter aircraft called the TFX (Tactical Fighter Experimental). Both services needed a platform that could carry a heavy weapons load at high speed over long distances. The USAF, however, was planning on arming its aircraft with bombs, not air-to-air missiles! The TFX subsequently evolved into the highly successful 'swing–wing' General Dynamics F-111A bomber, which would serve the air force well for almost 30 years. The same could not be said about the near-identical airframe that was foisted upon the US Navy in the form of the Grumman F-111B.

This aircraft soon proved to be totally unsuited to the fighter mission, being too

Defense Secretary Robert S McNamara played a major part in the development of the F-14's predecessor, the Grumman F-111B. The latter, based on the USAF's ultimately successful F-111 'swing-wing' tactical bomber, was an abject failure. (LBJ Library)

heavy due to the numerous aspects of its design that needed to be strengthened to make it fit for carrier operations. This in turn meant that the F-111B was too slow to be safely flown around 'the boat' in an operational configuration. This very point was bluntly driven home by Deputy Chief of Naval Operations (Air Warfare) Vice Admiral Tom Connolly during a Senate hearing on Capitol Hill by the Armed Services Committee into the future of the TFX on 4 March 1968. He told committee chairman Senator John Stennis, 'Mr Chairman, all the thrust in Christendom couldn't make a Navy fighter out of that airplane'. The TFX programme was eventually cancelled in December 1968.

In October of the previous year, having by then seen that the F-111B was 'falling well behind the power curve', Grumman

During July 1968, the US Navy conducted carrier suitability trials with the fifth F-111B prototype aboard USS Coral Sea (CVA-43) off the California coast. All flights were performed by Naval Aviators from the Naval Flight Test Center. (Grumman History Center via D Brown)

proposed to the US Navy that it could quickly produce a new airframe that incorporated the missile armament (AIM-54A), avionics, AN/AWG-9 weapon system and twin engines (Pratt & Whitney TF30 turbofans) of the F-111B. Called the Model 303, this design also featured a variable-geometry 'swing-wing'.

Grumman engineers had been secretly working on this proposal since the mid-1960s, and the US Navy was keen to proceed with a replacement for the F-111B. In July 1968 it issued a formal Request for Proposals to industry for a VFX (Heavier-than-air Fighter, Experimental). The US Navy's requirement stated that manufacturers should submit proposals for a tandem two-seat twin-engined aircraft that featured an advanced weapon control system, mixed short-, medium- and long-range missile armament consisting of AIM-54s, AIM-7s and AIM-9s and an integral Vulcan M61A 20 mm cannon.

Five companies, including Grumman, responded to the VFX competition, and on 14 January 1969 its Model 303E was selected as the winning design. Grumman was awarded a contract for the construction of six research, development, test and evaluation (RDT&E) aircraft and some 463 production examples

The time has come to provide our air wings with a fighter designed from scratch for air superiority. The F-14 is all fighter. Multi-mission capability has not been permitted to dilute the original concept, or degrade the performance required to out-fly and out-fight any aircraft encountered.'
Capt L S 'Scotty' Lamoreaux
F-14 Programme project coordinator, 1969

Did you know?
Although a modern warplane is the creation of many minds, the Tomcat was effectively the brainchild of a single man – Mike Pelehach. He became Grumman's vice president and F-14 programme director.

This full-scale mock-up of Grumman's Design 303E looks remarkably like the final Tomcat configuration settled on by the US Navy. (Grumman History Center via D Brown)

Having wasted ten years on the stillborn Missileer and F-111B, the US Navy was anxious to make up time with the F-14. It therefore stipulated in its contract entered into with Grumman that the first RDT&E aircraft would make its maiden flight on or before 31 January 1971. With the 'Iron Works' confident that it would be selected for the VFX programme, the company had already started the fabrication of minor components in December 1968. By May 1969 a full-scale mock-up had been assembled at Grumman's Bethpage facility that bore a striking resemblance to the finished fighter. The legend that would become the Tomcat was now nearing completion.

for frontline service with the both the US Navy and US Marine Corps. At this time the service designation F-14 was also bestowed upon the new fighter.

Production of all 712 Tomcats built by Grumman was undertaken at the company's Calverton facility on Long Island. The aircraft's external appearance altered very little during the 22 years that F-14s rolled down the assembly line, its overall shape having been settled on by programme director Mike Pelehach and his team as early as January 1968.

'When creating the most advanced air superiority fighter in history', Pelehach recalled, 'our studies boiled down to eight specific design numbers: 303-60, 303A, 303B, 303C, 303D, 303E, 303F and 303G.

The first RDT&E aircraft is seen here during the very early stages of its second flight on 30 December 1970. The aircraft spectacularly crashed on short finals to Grumman's Calverton facility shortly after this photograph was taken when it suffered a triple hydraulic failure. Both crewmen safely ejected. (Grumman History Center via Tailhook)

We were close to the real thing with design 303-60, which had podded engines and a high variable-sweep wing like our eventual winning design, 303E. But it was more an assemblage of reasonable goals than a mature blend of aerodynamics, structures, electronics and airframe systems'.

Assembly of the first RDT&E airframe proceeded well thanks to Grumman's years of development work firstly on the TFX and now the VFX. Aspects of the aircraft's design had been thoroughly trialled and tested prior to the first prototype being built. Four years of engineering and wind tunnel work had gone into developing the F-14's unique air inlet and engine/exhaust nozzle layout for example.

Central to the fighter's projected performance was its 'swing wings', which could be either automatically or manually varied in sweep, camber, area and aspect ratio at angles between 20 and 60 degrees. The aircraft's performance could therefore be maximised in a variety of flight envelopes thanks to the wing's variable sweep. In reality, this meant that the F-14 crew could crank its wings fully forward so as to 'turn and burn' in a dogfight with the most agile adversary, and then sweep them fully back to achieve eye-watering speeds when tasked with intercepting cruise missile-carrying bombers.

Grumman commenced taxi trials with the first RDT&E aircraft (BuNo 157980) at Calverton on 14 December 1970, and exactly one week later project test pilot William 'Bob' Miller and company chief test pilot Robert Smythe made the Tomcat's maiden flight. The latter was little more than a short test hop with the wings in fixed forward position. On 30 December both pilots took off on what was planned to be a more testing second flight. Having completed stability and control assessments with the landing gear down, the crew 'cleaned up' the airframe and slowly increased their speed to 207 mph (332 kmh).

Some 25 minutes into the mission, the pilot of one of the chase aircraft shadowing BuNo 157980 reported that smoke was coming from the Tomcat. Seconds later Miller radioed Calverton that the jet's primary hydraulic system had failed – the 'smoke' trailing from the jet was actually hydraulic fluid pouring from ruptured tubing. Switching to a back-up system, the crew got to within a mile (1.6 km) of the runway before the flight hydraulic system also failed and both pilots were forced to

eject a mere 25 ft (8 m) above the trees that surrounded Calverton.

An investigation of the charred wreckage revealed that the cause of the crash had been a resonance-induced fracture of the titanium hydraulic lines, and this failure had been worsened by a loose mounting connection. Stainless steel was duly adopted in place of titanium on all subsequent RDT&E and production F-14s. One positive aspect to emerge from the crash was the strength of the jet's wing box, which anchored its 'swing wings'.

RDT&E aircraft No 6 was delivered to the Pacific Missile Test Center (PMTC) at Point Mugu on 18 December 1971. Heavily involved in missile separation and weapons tests – it is seen here firing AIM-54 practice rounds – the aircraft managed to shoot itself down during AIM-7E-2 trials on 20 June 1972. The weapon pitched up on firing and ruptured several fuel cells, which duly ignited. The crew successfully ejected. (US Navy)

Seen here carrying a full load of AIM-54s, RDT&E aircraft No 11 of the PMTC was assigned to the Point Mugu unit in March 1972 for systems compatibility tests (US Navy)

Combining electro-beam welding and high strength titanium, the box was some 900 lbs lighter than the bolt-up steel structure used by the F-111. The box fitted to BuNo 157980 was recovered intact from the crash site, having buried itself some six feet (1.8 m) under the ground.

Although the hydraulic line fix had been quick to implement, the loss of the first aircraft delayed flight-testing until 24 May 1971, when the second RDT&E jet made its first flight. Eventually, some 20 early-build aircraft would participate in the flight trials programme for the Tomcat, which was soon brought back on schedule. The No 2 aircraft performed low-speed handling and crucial stall/spin trials, No 3 conducted performance envelope expanding flights with increasing loads and speeds, whilst Nos 4, 5 and 6 went to the Naval Missile

Center at NAS Point Mugu, California, for operational test and evaluation. Here, they conducted weapons trials, with No 4 being the first F-14 to be fitted with a functioning AN/AWG-9/AIM-54 system. No 6 was lost during AIM-7 separation trials on 20 June 1972.

No 7 became Grumman's test aircraft for the F-14B, fitted with Pratt & Whitney F401-PW-400 turbofan engines, No 8 was

Aircraft No 10 achieved the milestone of carrying out the first carrier launch and trap, aboard USS *Forrestal* (CVA-59), on 15 June 1972. The vessel was sailing some 115 miles off the coast of Virginia, the F-14 having

the first of several Tomcats delivered to the Naval Air Test Center (NATC) at NAS Patuxent River, Maryland. The follow-on RDT&E airframes were split between the NATC and Point Mugu's operational test and evaluation squadron VX-4, with nine Tomcats having been assigned to various test programmes by December 1971. That same month Cdr George White became the first US Navy test pilot to fly the F-14.

RDT&E aircraft No 10 is carefully craned aboard USS Forrestal *(CVA-59) whilst the vessel is alongside in Norfolk Navy Yard on 13 June 1972. The aircraft carried out the F-14's first launch and trap from the ship two days later off the coast of Virginia. (Grumman History Center)*

RDT&E aircraft No 10 completes an early cat shot from CVA-59 during initial carrier operations for the F-14 in June 1972. (Grumman History Center)

been craned aboard in Norfolk two days earlier. By the 28th of that month the jet had completed its initial carrier operations following three catapult launches, two arrested landings, 13 touch-and-goes and three intentional wave-offs. Two days later test pilot Bob Miller was killed in this aircraft when it crashed into Chesapeake Bay while he was practising for an airshow.

For the duration of the trials period, Grumman employed a small fleet of KA-6 Intruder tankers to extend the Tomcat missions. It also made use of an automated telemetry system to relay in-flight data to the ground in real-time for rapid evaluation. These aspects of the test programme, together with integrated service trials and operational instruction for ground and aircrews, combined to cut 18 months off the projected development time for the F-14. This meant that the first production aircraft reached the Pacific Fleet's fleet replacement squadron VF-124 at NAS Miramar, California, in October 1972.

As previously mentioned, all 712 Tomcats constructed by Grumman between 1970 and 1992 were assembled at the company's Calverton facility. The actual process of manufacture took place at several locations by a number of sub-contracting companies. Eventually, all the various parts would come together at Calverton's Plant 6, which served as an assembly hall for the A-6 Intruder and EA-6B Prowler, as well as the F-14.

Grumman employed a modular concept when it came to Tomcat assembly, some seven stations being responsible for different aspects of this process. Station A was where construction started, with the mating of the nacelle assembly to the forward/centre-fuselage module, mating of the aft fuselage and nacelle assemblies, fitting of the inlet/glove assemblies and attachment of the

A wingless F-14A fuselage is carefully craned into position at Station A within the assembly hall at Plant 6 in the mid-1970s. All the various parts built by sub-contractors for Grumman would come together at its huge Calverton plant. (Grumman History Center)

More F-14As are seen moving through Stations One and Two at Calverton's Plant 6. As this photograph clearly shows, the Tomcat was a large and complex machine. (Grumman History Center)

cockpit canopy. Moving on to Station One, the aircraft had its vertical tail surfaces and main undercarriage members added. Wings and engines were installed at Station Two, with rigging and the testing of flight control systems being carried out at Station Three. Engineers at the latter station also oversaw the installation of the AN/AWG-9, Central Air Data Computer and other mission-optimised avionics. This equipment was tested at Station Four, after which the completed aircraft was wheeled outside for engine runs and fuel flow calibration with technicians from Station Five. The jet was painted at Station Six and the weapons racks added and the weapon system tested (including firing the cannon) at Station Seven.

Having passed along the production line, the aircraft was cleared for flight and taken aloft by Grumman test pilots. After a thorough workout, the brand new F-14 was handed over to the US Navy's Calverton-based acceptance team, which also flew it, prior to despatch to a Fleet unit either at NAS Miramar or NAS Oceana, Virginia.

Despite being hailed as the most advanced fighter of its time when production of the F-14 commenced in 1970, its construction was largely conventional. The most important part of the aircraft was its single-cell titanium wing box, which was truly cutting edge. It was fabricated from 33 machined parts fused together via electron beam welding – the first time that this process had been applied to the construction of a modern combat aircraft. The 22 ft (6.7 m) long box transmitted its wing loadings to the fuselage via two sets of wing pivots. It also served as an integral fuel tank. The box was attached to the fuselage via four pin joints. Titanium alloy was also used in the construction of the two annular, spherical bearings that made up the wing pivots, these being Teflon-coated. The pivots were then bolted to the wing box.

The fuselage was assembled around conventionally machined steel frames. The latter was used for the aft fuselage and undercarriage support frame, as well as for the spectacle beam onto which the rear

'I don't believe that anyone who has ever flown the F-14A Tomcat would argue with the statement that the airplane's greatest weakness was the engine. The match between the airframe and the engine was a bad one. For the most part, efforts to improve the engine in the F-14A were of the band-aid variety. That is to say they tended to fix the symptoms rather than the problem.'
Rear Admiral Paul T Gillcrist
Commander, Fighter Airborne Early Warning Wings, Pacific Fleet, NAS Miramar

engine and stabiliser mounts were attached. Bonded honeycomb panels were also widely used for fuselage skinning throughout the aircraft as a weight-saving device, although the aft 'hot section' panels near the engine were made of titanium. The latter material could better withstand the high temperatures found in these areas, as well as being

corrosion resistant. Titanium was also used for the upper and lower wing skins, engine intakes, hydraulic lines, main and aft fuselage longerons and the engine support beam.

Elsewhere, bonded honeycomb material formed the glove vanes in the wing leading edges, the inlet duct sidewalls, the leading and trailing edges of the wings and the moveable control surfaces. The jet's distinctive twin tails also made use of honeycomb sandwich skinning. The horizontal tail surface skins, dubbed 'tailerons' by Naval Aviators, were made up of boron-epoxy composite materials. This was the first time that any Western production aircraft had used composites for loading-bearing structures.

The original engine fitted into the F-14A was the 12,350-lb (5,600-kg) thrust Pratt & Whitney TF30-P-412 axial-flow turbofan, which was an improved version of the TF30-P-12 that had been rigorously tested in the F-111B. Even before the first prototype had flown, Grumman knew that this powerplant had some serious flaws. It was underpowered – despite thrust increasing to 20,900 lb (7,400 kg) when in afterburner – and was particularly susceptible to compressor stalls if intake airflow was disturbed. The stalling problem was further amplified by the fact that the TF30s were widely spaced on the Tomcat. If an engine stalled whilst the aircraft was in afterburner, the sudden onset of asymmetric thrust could cause the nose to slice (rotation in yaw) so violently that the jet suffered a flat spin departure which was often impossible for the pilot to recover from.

Designed in the late 1950s, the TF30 was originally only meant to power the RDT&E airframes and the first 61 production F-14As. From 1973 onward all new Tomcats (as well as those A-models already delivered) would be fitted with the Pratt & Whitney F401-PW-400, which had 30 per cent more thrust than the TF30. This variant was to be designated the F-14B (not to be confused with the F-14B that entered fleet service in the late 1980s). However, by the time the new engine commenced flight-testing in a modified A-model, the Tomcat was running way over budget.

As early as April 1971, Grumman had been warned by the Department of Defense that costs would have to be cut or the F-14

may be cancelled. Rampant inflation made the problem worse, as Grumman struggled to meet the fixed-price stipulation in the contract that it had signed with the US Navy in 1969. With funding tight and some members of Congress calling for the Tomcat programme to be terminated, Deputy Defense Secretary David Packard had little choice but to perform merciless major surgery on the project in May 1971 that saw the cancelling of the F401 engine (which was proving too complicated and expensive for Fleet use in the short term). Both the F-14B and improved F-14C also fell victim to budget cuts at this point.

RDT&E aircraft No 7 became the test bed for the promising Pratt & Whitney F401-PW-400 engine, which the US Navy had hoped to fit to all of its Tomcats in due course. Designated the F-14B, this aircraft and the F401 fell victim to chronic cost overruns in the Tomcat programme and were jointly cancelled in May 1971. This photograph was taken after the aircraft had been resurrected in 1981 as the General Electric F101-powered F-14B Super Tomcat. (Grumman History Center)

The Navy persevered with the TF30, and it took a decade before aircraft fitted with the modestly improved -414 started to reach the fleet – the final -412 engine was retired in the summer of 1979. The more reliable and durable -414A was fitted into the Tomcat from early 1981, and this version remained the powerplant for all A-model aircraft until the jets' retirement in 2004.

By then more than 50 Tomcats, worth $1.5 billion, had been lost through engine-related problems – primarily compressor stalls caused as a result of the jet being at high angles of attack when the fighter was being vigorously manoeuvred during air combat training. Such failures caused high profile Navy Secretary, and Naval Aviator, John F Lehman to tell Congress in 1984 that the 'F-14/TF30 combination was the worst engine/airframe mismatch we have had in many years. The TF30 is simply a terrible engine'.

By the mid-1980s Grumman had been given approval by the US Navy to look into re-engining a number of F-14As with the General Electric F110-GE-400 turbofan. This powerplant would duly be fitted into the F-14B (formerly F-14A+) and the F-14D, and both variants are described in detail later in this volume.

Despite being the most complex fighter aircraft ever to operate from a carrier flightdeck, and plagued by financial wrangling and cost overruns, the F-14 attained service entry on 8 October 1972 – just 21 months after the Tomcat had made its maiden flight. The first production machine had flown in May of that year, and five months later VF-124 took delivery of its first Tomcat at NAS Miramar. This signalled a high point in the jet's development, as it showed that the F-14 was progressing from being an aircraft undergoing testing to a fighter capable of performing its designated mission.

VF-124 was not an operational fighter unit, however. It was a Fleet Replacement Squadron charged with providing tuition in all aspects of the aircraft it was assigned for the air- and groundcrew who would ultimately operate the jet at sea. Staffed by seasoned Naval Aviators drawn from the fighter community on both coasts, the unit's first job was to train the instructors who would in turn be tasked with drawing up a formal syllabus for the future tuition of frontline air crew and maintainers. VF-124 also had to manage the transition process for fleet units that would be swapping their F-4s or F-8s for F-14s.

The flow of aircraft to Miramar from Calverton was slow to start with, and it was not until the spring of 1973 that the unit

This aircraft (BuNo 158617) was the very first Tomcat to be assigned to VF-124 'Gunfighters' when it was temporarily loaned to the unit so that would-be F-14 instructors could gain experience on the new fleet fighter. Finally struck off charge in October 2003, the jet has been preserved in Allenton, Pennsylvania, by the Veterans of Foreign Wars Post 7293. (US Navy via Angelo Romano)

started training crews that were destined to join the Pacific Fleet's first F-14-equipped squadrons within its Fighter Airborne Early Warning Wings Pacific (FitAEWWingPac). The first two squadrons slated to introduce the jet to seagoing service were VF-1 and VF-2, which had been commissioned specially to fly the Tomcat at Miramar on 14 October 1972. By July 1973 both units had made sufficient progress in transitioning onto the jet to allow them to

take delivery of their own F-14As directly from Grumman. It would take until March 1974 for VF-1 and VF-2 to attain full unit strength of 12 jets apiece.

Assigned to Carrier Air Wing (CVW) 14, which was embarked in USS *Enterprise* (CVN-65) at the time, both units completed their carrier qualifications with the aircraft in the spring of 1974 and then deployed aboard the vessel for the Western Pacific (WestPac) on 17 September that same year. The cruise, which lasted until 20 May 1975, was relatively successful for the Tomcat units, as they got to expend live examples of all three missile types in the jet's inventory during training exercises, as well as flying combat air patrols (CAPs) over Saigon during the final stages of the US evacuation from South Vietnam, codenamed Operation *Frequent Wind*. Less successful was the fact that VF-1 lost two F-14s to engine fan blade failure, which in turn started uncontrollable fires, within the space of 12 days in early January 1975. Both jets crashed into the South China Sea, but the crews were recovered safely.

Despite these losses, and the units being forced to make around 100 engine changes each during the course of the cruise because of the TF30's chronic unreliability, VF-1 and VF-2 returned to Miramar with 3,000 flying hours under their belts. And, overall, the deployment was described by Rear Admiral Leonard A Snead, Commander FitAEWWingPac, as being 'the most singularly successful fleet introduction of a sophisticated aircraft the Navy has ever had'.

By the time these units were back home, the first two Atlantic Fleet squadrons –

VF-14 and VF-32 – were nearing readiness for their first operational deployment. In order to speed up the Tomcat's introduction to service, the US Navy had decided to transition the first four east coast fighter squadrons slated to receive the F-14 with VF-124 at Miramar. In late 1975, former Atlantic Fleet F-4 FRS VF-101 received its first F-14s. The unit operated both fighter types until August 1977, when VF-101 passed the last of its Phantom IIs on to VF-171 and focused exclusively on Tomcat

The first two frontline units to receive the F-14A were VF-1 'Wolfpack' and VF-2 'Bounty Hunters', both of which were commissioned specially to fly the Tomcat at Miramar on 14 October 1972. Amongst the first aircraft issued to VF-1 was this F-14A, BuNo 158993, which remained in fleet service until retired in October 1990. (Robert L Lawson via Tailhook)

> VF-1's Tomcats were amongst the most colourful F-14s flown by Fighter Airborne Early Warning Wings Pacific. This aircraft (BuNo 159000) was photographed on the ramp at Miramar shortly after its delivery to the 'Wolfpack' from Calverton in early 1974. (David F Brown)

> A section of VF-1 F-14As formate with two F-106As from the 2nd Fighter Weapons Squadron/325th Fighter Weapons Wing after a session of air combat manoeuvring (ACM) in the Southern California Operations area. Below them is San Diego (right) and Coronado Island (left), the latter being home to NAS North Island. (US Navy)

training in support of east coast fighter squadrons.

Formerly equipped with F-4Js, VF-14 and VF-32 returned home to NAS Oceana from

California in the late summer of 1974. After a further nine months of intensive training with the Tomcat, they joined up with the rest of CVW-1 aboard USS *John F Kennedy* (CV-67) and departed Norfolk, Virginia, on 28 June 1975. The carrier headed across the Atlantic for a seven-month deployment that set the tone for future operations for Oceana-based Tomcat units during the Cold War. CV-67 spent much of its time in the eastern Mediterranean, and also exercised extensively with NATO forces.

Atlantic Fleet units VF-142 and VF-143 followed VF-14 and VF-32 through Miramar's 'Tomcat School' during the latter half of 1974, swapping their F-4Js for F-14As. Both squadrons would have to wait until April 1976, however, before they headed to the Mediterranean with CVW-6 aboard USS *America* (CV-66). The

cruise highlight came in late July when Tomcats from both units provided CAP for US Marine Corps helicopters tasked with evacuating 300+ US civilians from the Lebanese capital Beirut after the outbreak of a bloody civil war.

Having completed the transition of the first four Atlantic Fleet Tomcat units, VF-124 switched its attention back to FitAEWWingPac and conversion of the last two frontline F-8 squadrons in the US Navy. VF-24 and VF-211 had flown the Crusader

VF-14 'Tophatters' and sister-squadron VF-32 'Swordsmen' were the first Atlantic Fleet fighter units to transition to the F-14A. They undertook their conversion with VF-124 at Miramar, where this aircraft was photographed between flights in May 1975. (Angelo Romano)

►
VF-32's storeless 'Gypsy 211' is shot off CV-67's waist catapult four during the Tomcat's maiden Mediterranean cruise in the autumn of 1975. Retired in September 1994, this aircraft has been an exhibit aboard USS Yorktown (CVS-10), which is part of the Patriots Point Naval and Maritime Museum in South Carolina, for many years. (Angelo Romano)

Did you know?

VF-84 was the first unit to deploy with TARPS-capable photo-reconnaisance Tomcats in August 1981, embarking three jets in USS *Nimitz* (CVN-68).

since 1959, and having completed their ninth cruise with the jet, they commenced their transition to the F-14A in the autumn of 1975. Both squadrons were assigned to CVW-9 and undertook their first WestPac embarked in USS *Constellation* (CV-64) in April 1977. Six months later, VF-114 and VF-213 completed their transition from the F-4J to the F-14A and embarked in USS *Kitty Hawk* (CV-63) with the rest of CVW-11 for their first WestPac – the vessel replaced CV-64 on deployment.

1977 was a busy year for Grumman and the US Navy, for in December VF-41 and VF-84 set out on their first cruise with the Atlantic Fleet, having been the first units to complete their transition with VF-101 at Oceana. The latter unit had started both squadrons' conversion from the F-4N to F-14A in April 1976, VF-101

initially receiving considerable help from VF-124. Following this flurry of transitions, both FRSs would enjoy a brief respite from converting Phantom II units to Tomcats until VF-124 welcomed VF-51 and VF-111 to the classroom in early 1978. Part of CVW-15, they eventually took F-14As on their first WestPac in May 1979.

Most deployments during the latter half of the 1970s followed a predictable pattern, with carriers typically spending around six months on cruise in the Pacific or Mediterranean. During this time Tomcat units could expect to exercise with foreign air arms, as well as spending countless hours on CAP providing protection for the carrier battle group. One of the missions F-14 crews soon became familiar with was 'Bear' hunting. Soviet Antonov, Ilyushin and Tupolev long-range reconnaissance aircraft would routinely probe the Tomcat CAPs in an effort to get close to their carriers so as to take photographs and collect electronic signals data. Amongst the many Naval Aviators to intercept these aircraft during this period was Lt John Skogsberg of VF-14, who recalled:

When the Soviet reconnaissance aircraft were able to find the carrier, they could get pretty much as close as they wanted. Short of ramming them or shooting them

Crews with dogfighting experience in the F-4 and F-8 were taught how best to use the F-14 in close aerial combat. A brand new Tomcat from VF-143 with a T-38A Talon from VF-43 over a training range near MCAS Yuma, Arizona. (Robert L Lawson via Tailhook)

Did you know?

In November 1976 an F-14 and its Phoenix missile were recovered from 1,900 ft down 75 miles northwest of the Orkneys eight weeks after its loss over the side of CV-67 in a marshalling accident. This was done at great cost to the US Navy to prevent the kit falling into Soviet hands.

down, there was no practical way for us to keep them away.

Our goals were to have them continuously escorted any time they were within about 200 miles of the ship – sometimes much farther – and to try to

This was the first F-14A assigned to VF-114 'Aardvarks' in 1976. It is seen here departing Miramar having blown both main gear tyres performing a no-flaps take-off at the start of its display at the 1976 NAS Miramar airshow. (Robert L Lawson via Tailhook)

In May 1977, a handful of F-14As from VF-1 and VF-2 were repainted in disruptive two-grey splinter camouflage, dubbed the Ferris scheme (after noted aviation artist Keith Ferris), to test whether this made the fighters more difficult to spot in combat. This aircraft was VF-2's 'Bullet 200'. These schemes had been abandoned by year-end. (David F Brown)

always, as the escort, be in every picture they might take of the carrier. In the main, the Tu-95/142 'Bear' and Tu-16 'Badger' crews played nice, but there were stories of Il-38 'Mays' getting very low and slow to try to give the escorts problems.

With the overthrow of the Shah of Iran in 1979, the US Navy found itself patrolling the narrow waters of the North Arabian Gulf (NAG). Carriers from both the Pacific and Atlantic Fleets would take it in turns to spend time on 'Gonzo Station', as this operating area was soon irreverently dubbed. The invasion of Iran by Iraq in September 1980 further heightened tensions in this oil-rich region, and Tomcat units were kept busy patrolling the airspace overhead carrier battle groups operating in-theatre. Indeed, US Navy Tomcats would remain a familiar sight in the skies over the NAG for the next 27 years.

Despite the US Navy's operational focus having shifted to the Middle East, Atlantic Fleet carriers continued to routinely patrol in the eastern Mediterranean whilst assigned to the Sixth Fleet. And it was here on 19

August 1981 that the Tomcat unexpectedly won its battle spurs in its intended role as a fighter. USS *Nimitz* (CVN-68), with CVW-8 embarked, was conducting a two-day missile launching exercise against drone targets operating in international waters off the coast of Libya, and the government of the latter country claimed that much of the range area in which the drones were flying was its territorial waters. The US government refuted this, stating that it was only prepared to recognise the traditional three-mile limit.

The first day of the exercise (18 August) had seen close to 50 incursions into the missile-firing zone by Libyan Arab Republic Air Force (LARAF) aircraft, which ended with air combat manoeuvring (ACM) between the latter and F-14s from VF-41 and VF-84, as well as F-4Js from USS *Forrestal* (CV-59). On the morning of the 19th two Sukhoi Su-22 'Fitter-J' fighters took on a pair of Tomcats from VF-41, and the pilot of one of the LARAF fighters made the mistake of launching a single 'Atoll' heat-seeking missile at the US Navy jets as all four aircraft converged on each other. The weapon failed to guide, however, since it had been launched outside of its operational envelope. Following the strict rules of engagement observed by US Navy aircrew at that time, which stated that they could only engage the enemy if first

Fleet Replacement Squadron VF-101 'Grim Reapers' was the Tomcat training unit for the Atlantic Fleet. The squadron initially operated F-14s alongside its large fleet of F-4s from Oceana, but in August 1977 VF-101 passed the last of its Phantom IIs on to VF-171 and focused exclusively on Tomcat training. This aircraft was one of more than 20 F-14As assigned to the 'Grim Reapers' in 1979.

➤

For Tomcat crews charged with protecting the fleet, some of the most exciting missions during the Cold War were the interceptions they flew against Soviet long-range reconnaissance aircraft attempting to take photographs of US Navy carriers and collect electronic signals data emanating from them. This Il-38 'May' was photographed from an RF-8G Crusader whilst being shadowed by an F-14A from VF-41 'Black Aces' in the Indian Ocean in January 1980. The Ilyushin was shadowing the aircrafts' carrier USS Nimitz (CVN-68). (US Navy)

fired upon, the Naval Aviators in the VF-41 jets each shot a 'Fitter' down with a single AIM-9L.

On a more mundane note, VF-11 and VF-31 made their first Tomcat deployment following their transition from the Phantom II in January 1982 when the units joined CVW-3 aboard USS *John F Kennedy* (CV-67). In December of that same year VF-33 and VF-102 also embarked on their first Mediterranean cruise with CVW-1 in USS *America* (CV-66).

Tomcats operating with the Atlantic Fleet would see more combat in 1983, although this time their primary weapon was the Tactical Air Reconnaissance Pod System (TARPS) rather than an air-to-air missile. With the retirement of the Vietnam-era RA-5C Vigilante and RF-8G Crusader from frontline service in 1980-81,

the US Navy needed a new carrier-based photo-reconnaissance platform. With its long range and high speed, the F-14 was chosen for the task. The development of TARPS had commenced in April 1976, with the 17.29 ft (5.27 m) long pod housing two cameras and an infrared reconnaissance sensor optimised for use at low-to-medium altitudes. Initially, just 50 F-14As had their rear right Phoenix station wired for TARPS operation, these aircraft then being spread amongst the frontline force. Only one squadron in an air wing would be assigned the TARPS mission, and the first pods (weighing in at a hefty 1760 lb/798 kg) were used operationally by VF-84 in late 1981.

By the time VF-32 was tasked with flying TARPS missions over Grenada in October 1983 and Lebanon two months later, the unit was highly proficient with the system. Flying from USS *Independence* (CV-62), it often relied on VF-14 to CAP these potentially hazardous flights. In Grenada, the TARPS imagery provided US Marines and Army Rangers with intelligence on troop movements and gun emplacements ahead of the invasion of the

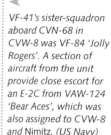

VF-41's sister-squadron aboard CVN-68 in CVW-8 was VF-84 'Jolly Rogers'. A section of aircraft from the unit provide close escort for an E-2C from VAW-124 'Bear Aces', which was also assigned to CVW-8 and Nimitz. (US Navy)

Armed with six AIM-54A training rounds, denoted by their blue stripes (live rounds have yellow stripes), this F-14A participated in VF-32's final CVW-1 Mediterranean cruise embarked in CV-67 in 1980-81. (US Navy)

Caribbean island, codenamed Operation *Urgent Fury*. In Lebanon, VF-32 flew 30+ TARPS missions over Druse and Syrian gun positions, as well as carrying out a Bomb

Chained down to the deck of CVN-68, VF-41's 'Fast Eagle 107' boasts a single Su-22 kill marking below its windscreen. This aircraft, flown by Lts Larry Muczynski and Dave Anderson, got the second of two Libyan Su-22 kills on 19 August 1981. The aircraft was lost on 25 October 1994 whilst assigned to VF-213 when it crashed attempting to land aboard USS Abraham Lincoln (CVN-72) off the coast of California. Its RIO, Lt Matthew Klemish, safely ejected, but pilot Lt Kara Hultgreen (one of the first two female pilots assigned to a US Navy fighter squadron) was killed. (Angelo Romano)

Damage Assessment mission following the ill-fated Alpha Strike on 4 December. The latter had been hastily arranged after a TARPS jet from CV-67's VF-31 had come under fire.

In April 1984, the last two east coast fighter units to transition to the Tomcat deployed for the first time, VF-74 and VF-103 joining CVW-17 embarked in USS *Saratoga* (CV-60). In February of the following year Miramar-based VF-21 and VF-154 headed out on their first WestPac with the F-14.

CVW-17's Tomcat units made the headlines in October 1985 when they were involved in the seizure of four Palestinian terrorists who had previously hijacked the Italian cruise liner *Achille Lauro* and murdered an elderly US passenger. Having found temporary refuge in Egypt, the terrorists were to be flown to sanctuary in Libya in an Egyptair Boeing 737. However, a precision night intercept by seven Tomcats from VF-74 and VF-103, coordinated by a USAF RC-135 and an AEW E-2C (the latter also from CVW-17), saw the airliner intercepted and forced to land at NAS Sigonella, on the Italian island of Sicily.

Libya felt the full force of US carrier air power once again in late March 1986

upon by SA-5 surface-to-air missile (SAM) batteries and anti-aircraft artillery, resulting in numerous air strikes being flown by A-6s, A-7s and F/A-18s from both vessels. No LARAF fighters were engaged on this occasion, however. On 15 April, USAF F-111s flying from bases in the UK attacked targets in Tripoli, with Tomcats from CV-60 and CV-66 provided CAP coverage.

Back in the US the last two frontline units to operate the F-14 started to receive aircraft in December 1986. VF-191 and VF-194 had been dormant fighter units since 1977-78, and they were established as part of the newly formed CVW-10 that was slated to embark in USS Independence (CV-62). Although both squadrons received a full complement of jets, and undertook a thorough work-up, they were disestablished in April 1988 when the

following its continued support for terrorism. USS America (CV-66) and USS Coral Sea (CV-43) were involved in Operation Prairie Fire, which sought to provoke the Libyan military into taking on the might of CVW-1 and CVW-13. CAPs by VF-33 and VF-102 (embarked in CV-66) were duly fired

Although the Tomcat had been in fleet service for a decade by the time this photograph was taken in early 1983, the test aircraft at VX-4 were kept busy evaluating systems and weapons upgrades for the F-14. The unit employed a varied fleet of fast jet types during this period, as this shot clearly shows. Leading the formation is a recently delivered F/A-18A, whilst bringing up the rear are single examples of the venerable F-4S Phantom II and TA-4J Skyhawk. (US Navy)

41

Pacific Fleet chopped CVW-10 following budget cuts. Surviving the latter, however, were reserve-manned F-14 units VF-201 and VF-202 of CVWR-20 and VF-301 and VF-302 of CVWR-30.

In March of the previous year, Grumman delivered the 557th, and last, production standard F-14A to the US Navy. It would now switch its attention to the F-14A+ (subsequently re-designated the F-14B) and the F-14D.

Five months later, on 8 August, two Tomcats from VF-21 – embarked in CV-64 – intercepted a pair of Islamic Republic of Iran Air Force (IRIAF) F-4Es from the 91st Tactical Fighter Wing (TFW) that were searching for Iraqi Mirage F 1s that had been attacking supertankers in the NAG. Fearing the Phantom IIs might attack US naval vessels, the Tomcat crews fired two Sparrow missiles at the Iranian fighters from head-on. Launched out of guidance parameters, one missile malfunctioned and

the other was easily evaded by the battle hardened F-4 crew.

IRIAF Phantom IIs again tangled with the US Navy on 18 April 1988 during Operation *Praying Mantis* – a one-day war-at-sea against Iranian frigates that had been attacking supertankers in the NAG. An F-4E was hit by a SAM fired from the cruiser USS *Wainwright* (CG-28), although it managed to limp back to base. Several hours later, a formation of Phantom IIs tried to intercept an E-2C launched from USS *Enterprise* (CVN-65), but they were warned off by two F-14As from VF-213.

In the last Cold War action of note involving the Tomcat, two jets from VF-32 succeeded in shooting down a pair of LARAF MiG-23 'Floggers' on 4 January 1989 during yet another 'freedom of navigation' exercise undertaken by Sixth Fleet off the

This VF-1 jet had to take the barricade aboard USS Ranger (CV-61) when its right main gear leg refused to lock down at the end of a sortie over the Indian Ocean in 1984. It was repaired and remained in fleet service until finally retired by VF-154 in 2003 following its participation in Operation Iraqi Freedom I. (US Navy)

VF-21 'Freelancers' and VF-154 'Black Knights' received their F-14As in 1983 and commenced their first WestPac with them aboard USS Constellation (CV-64) in 1985. Here, 'Nite 110' is attached to the launch shuttle of CV-64's waist catapult three, alongside it an F/A-18A from VFA-25. (US Navy)

In March 1986, VF-102's F-14As flew CAP missions from USS America (CV-66) for strike aircraft from CVW-1 that were sent to destroy Libyan surface-to-missile batteries that had fired on them. (US Navy via Peter Mersky)

In January 1987, the Naval Aviators of CVW-15 operated in some of the harshest conditions ever experienced by a US Navy air wing when CVN-70 conducted flight operations in the North Pacific. Here deckcrews struggle to sweep ice off the wings and fuselage of 'Sundowner 213' as the jet taxies out on the frozen deck. Bizarrely, the F-14A behind it features the NG tailcodes of CVW-9 and USS KITTY HAWK titling on its port fin!

The last two frontline Tomcat squadrons established by the US Navy were VF-191 'Satan's Kittens' and VF-194 'Red Lightnings', both of which were commissioned in December 1986. Part of CVW-10, which was formed as the 13th frontline air wing at the height of the Cold War, both units survived just 16 months before they were disestablished, having not made a single operational cruise. This particular aircraft was VF-194's CAG jet.

Heading out on an ACM training sortie from NAS Dallas, two VF-202 jets close up on their leader to allow the RIO to capture this wide-angle view aft of his F-14A. (US Navy via Peter Mersky)

Four US Navy Reserve units were issued with F-14As in 1985-87 – VF-201 'Hunters' and VF-202 'Superheats', both based at NAS Dallas, Texas, and VF-301 'Devil's Disciples' and VF-302 'Stallions' at NAS Miramar. VF-201 and VF-202 were assigned to Carrier Reserve Air Wing (CVWR) 20 of the Atlantic Fleet, whilst VF-301 and VF-302 were part of the Pacific Fleet's CVWR-30. Three of the units disestablished in 1994-95, but VF-201 soldiered on until it transitioned to F/A-18As in 1999. This 'Hunters' jet – the third-to-last A-model Tomcat built – is firing off an AIM-54C during an active duty training exercise. (US Navy)

Throughout the Tomcat's frontline service life, units flying the aircraft would send crews to the elite Naval Fighter Weapons School – better known as Topgun – for intensive training in ACM. This 'clean' VF-2 jet, wearing water-based temporary camouflage and carrying an ACM instrumentation pod on its left shoulder pylon, is flanked by a pair of F-16Ns from VF-126 'Bandits', which supported the Topgun school's training efforts from Miramar. (Lt Cdr Dave Baranek via Peter Mersky)

Libyan coastline. The Tomcats were flying CAP from CV-67 when an E-2C detected the two MiGs departing Bumbah air base. The latter, heading straight for the US Navy fighters, were picked at a range of 72 miles by the F-14s' AN/AWG-9 radar. The VF-32 jets duly performed an avoidance manoeuvre no fewer than four times in an attempt to avert a confrontation, but on each occasion the LARAF aircraft matched

their turns. When the jets were just 13 miles apart, a fighter controller aboard CV-67 gave the Tomcat crews permission to engage the MiG-23s, and two Sparrows were launched at the lead jet – it was quickly shot down. The second aircraft was destroyed by a Sidewinder after a third Sparrow had malfunctioned.

Despite the Tomcat evoking interest from a number of potential customers, the jet's expense and complexity meant that it was never going to enjoy the same kind of success that its predecessor, the F-4 Phantom II, had had in the export market. In fact the only country to buy the F-14 was also an operator of the McDonnell Douglas fighter.

Iran had long been one of the few allies of the US government in the Middle East. Its military was equipped with modern American hardware, and when Mohammad-Reza Pahlavi, Shah of Iran, expressed an interest in buying the Tomcat to President Richard Nixon during a trip to America in the summer of 1972, the deal was as good as done. Nevertheless,

This F-14A (BuNo 160299) was the first of 80 Tomcats built for the Imperial Iranian Air Force (IIAF). The aircraft made its first flight on 5 December 1975, and was delivered to Khatami air base in late January 1976. It subsequently downed at least two Iraqi aircraft while in service with the 81st and 82nd Tactical Fighter Squadrons during the Iran-Iraq War. Painted in the IIAF's distinctive 'Asia Minor' scheme, this aircraft was photographed during flight-testing from Grumman's Calverton plant. (Grumman History Center via Tom Cooper)

this controversial purchase, which also involved the acquisition of AIM-54A Phoenix missiles, was not approved by the US government until November 1973 owing to concerns in the State Department that there was discontent amongst the Iranian populace over the Shah's excessive spending on weaponry.

During the evaluation phase of the F-14, the Imperial Iranian Air Force (IIAF) also tested McDonnell Douglas' rival F-15 Eagle, but found that the Tomcat's AN/AWG-9 and AIM-54 pairing were unmatched when it came to long range detection and interception of incoming hostile aircraft. The latter, in Iran's case, were Soviet air force MiG-25R 'Foxbat' reconnaissance aircraft that had been regularly overflying the country safe in the knowledge that they were immune from interception.

Having received US approval for the deal, which was codenamed Project *Persian King*, the Iranians ordered 30 F-14As, spare parts, replacement engines and a complete armament package (including 424 AIM-54As) on 7 January 1974. Six months later a second order was placed for a further 50 F-14As and 290 Phoenix missiles. The overall bill for *Persian King* totalled $2 billion, which at the time was the highest value single foreign military equipment sale in US history.

This order would ultimately save both the Tomcat and Grumman itself, for in August 1974 US Congress halted the supply of funds to the company due to spiralling cost overruns on the jets being built for the US Navy. Desperate to get his F-14s, the Shah instructed the Iranian bank Melli to lend Grumman the money

Did you know?
On 13 September 1980, an IRIAF F-14 from the 81st Tactical Fighter Squadron shot down an IrAF MiG-23MS with an AIM-54. This encounter was the first time that two 'swing-wing' aircraft had fought each other in aerial combat. The destruction of the MiG also gave the Phoenix missile its first combat victory.

necessary for it to complete the IIAF order. He also encouraged other investors to underwrite loans to the company, allowing Grumman to weather the financial storm and keep the Tomcat production line open until 1992.

The F-14s supplied to Iran were virtually identical to the aircraft being delivered by Grumman to the US Navy at that time, and their Phoenix missiles were also very similar to those in the fleet. Indeed, with

'As a former F-4 pilot, I found the F-14A light years ahead right from the start of my training. I had no problem in leaving my Phantom II squadron for a new Tomcat unit. I loved the Phantom II, but learned to love the F-14A even more.'
Capt Javed, 81st Tactical Fighter Squadron
IIAF

the latter, only their electronic counter-countermeasures (ECCM) suites were downgraded so as to make the missiles less effective in combat against US-built aircraft and their ECM systems.

The first IIAF aircraft made its maiden flight on 5 December 1975, and late the following month the first three Tomcats to reach Iran arrived at Tehran (Mehrabad) air base. Most F-14s would be operated by the 8th TFW from the new facility in the

desert near Esfahan known as Khatami. The aircraft were flown by IIAF aircrew (all with F-4 experience) that had received training at either VF-124 or VF-101 in 1974-75. Additional support was supplied by US Navy instructors on secondment in Iran, while technical help was provided to IIAF groundcrews by engineers from Grumman and Hughes.

By July 1978 79 of the 80 Tomcats ordered had reached Iran, with the final jet being retained in the US by Grumman for fitment with a USAF-style flying boom refuelling receptacle. The IIAF had also received 284 of the 714 AIM-54As that it had ordered, but the rest failed to materialise following the overthrow of the Shah in early 1979 as part of Iran's Islamic Revolution. US technical support was also pulled out at around this time, and the

F-14 crews from Tactical Fighter Base 8 pose with one of their aircraft at Khatami in 1985-86. Despite severe maltreatment by the revolutionary regime, which branded these men the 'Shah's pilots', they remained determined to defend their country by fighting the IrAF whenever the opportunity arose. (via Tom Cooper)

Did you know?
At least three IRIAF F-14 pilots claimed five or more aerial victories to give them ace status in the Tomcat during the first Gulf War with Iraq.

War-weary F-14A 3-6060 photographed on display in Tehran in the early 1990s surrounded by other military hardware used in the Iran-Iraq conflict. (via Tom Cooper)

The F-14 closest to the camera is armed with a red-finned MIM-23 I-HAWK surface-to-air missile modified during Project Sky Hawk to allow it to be fired from a Tomcat. Four jets from the 82nd TFS received this modification in 1985-86, and although a number of firings were successfully made and two IrAF fighters possibly shot down, Sky Hawk was discontinued after the Iran-Iraq war ended in 1988. (IRIAF)

Islamic Republic Party that now ruled Iran arrested numerous IIAF aircrew (many of who were assigned to the Tomcat) that it claimed were the 'Shah's pilots'. Many more fled the country, as did a number of F-14 groundcrew. Training of replacements also ground to a halt, and the bulk of the Tomcat force remained unserviceable well into 1980.

This situation changed in September of that year when Iraq invaded Iran to signal the start of the first Gulf War. The F-14 would play an increasingly important role in this conflict, as more aircraft were returned to service. Many of the pilots that had been languishing in jails awaiting their execution were also freed and told to fight for their country. Their experience soon came to the fore, and between September 1980 and July 1988, no fewer than 159 Iraqi aircraft fell victim to the F-14. A further 34 claims remain unconfirmed.

The IRIAF had used all the weapons available to the Tomcat during the eight-year conflict, with the performance of the AIM-54A being particularly noteworthy. The clandestine supply of parts from the US and reverse engineering programmes instigated by the Iranians helped keep both the F-14 and its complex radar and weapons systems operable, although by the latter stages of the conflict the Tomcat force was beginning to suffer from reduced availability. It also experienced a handful of losses in 1988 to IrAF Mirage F 1EQs equipped with the very latest French air-to-air missiles that had been trained to lock onto radar emissions from the F-14's AN/AWG-9. By war's end, it is estimated that

Displaying the blue-grey camouflage scheme adopted by the IRIAF for its F-14s in the mid-1990s, 3-6024 was a star exhibit at the 'Holy War of Defence' exhibition staged in Tehran in November 2001. This machine not only shot down at least six IrAF fighters, it also participated in the pursuit of a Soviet MiG-25R in the late summer of 1978, which led to the termination of all 'Foxbat' overflights of Iran. (via Tom Cooper)

3-6058 on short finals after a post-overhaul check flight. It was one of three F-14As that had overhauls by Iranian Aircraft Industries at Mehrabad after the IRIAF was put on alert in December 2008 amid fears that Israel was planning an attack on Iranian nuclear installations. (Mohammad Razzazan via Tom Cooper)

Closing on a KC-707 with its refuelling probe and glove vanes extended, this aircraft was photographed whilst on patrol over northern Iran in early 2009 (IRIAF via Tom Cooper)

between 12 and 16 Tomcats had been lost to enemy action.

The F-14 still remains a key weapon in the IRIAF today, with most surviving airframes having completed a complex overhaul and modification programme with Iranian Aircraft Industries (IACI) at its Mehrabad plant. New weapons (some Soviet in origin), datalinks and communication systems have all been added to the aircraft. The venerable Phoenix missile has also benefited from an upgrade that has seen its capability boosted to match the performance of the US Navy's AIM-54C variant.

It is unknown exactly how many Tomcats remain in service with the IRIAF, but formations totalling up to 25 jets have been periodically tracked by US AWACS aircraft operating in Iraq since 2003.

As previously detailed in this volume, the F-14A Tomcat was only meant to be an interim version of the aircraft constructed in limited numbers (36 airframes) so as to introduce the jet to frontline service. The bulk of the 700+ airframes on order for the US Navy were supposed to built as F-14Bs, fitted with more powerful F401 engines, and F-14Cs, which would have had the new engines and a revised digital avionics suite that could have turned the jet into an all-weather air-to-ground attack platform. Chronic budget overruns saw both variants cancelled very early on in the programme and left the US Navy equipped exclusively with the TF30-powered F-14A.

There was very little money available to update the Tomcat during the first decade of its fleet service, and by 1982 the jet was beginning to lag behind its contemporaries in the west (and, to a lesser degree, in the Soviet bloc) in four key areas. First and

The original F-14B, which had briefly flown with Pratt & Whitney F401 engines fitted in 1971, was removed from storage ten years later to serve once again as an engine test bed for the General Electric F101-DFE. The latter powerplant, which evolved into the F110-GE-400, was eventually adopted by the US Navy for the F-14A+ (redesigned the F-14B in May 1991) and the F-14D. The aircraft, christened the Super Tomcat, was further modified to serve as the D-model prototype in 1986, before being retired. It is presently on display aboard USS Intrepid (CV-11) as part of the Sea, Air & Space Museum in New York City.

foremost, the TF30 engine was still causing the Fleet major problems both in terms of reliability and overall performance. The maintainability of the jet, and its systems (specifically its dated, valve-driven fire control system), was also poor. The AN/AWG-9 and AIM-54 had also by now become more susceptible to jamming by improved Soviet ECM expertise. Finally, the Tomcat lacked the high-speed multiplex digital databuses present in aircraft such as the F-15C, F-16 and F/A-18. The latter would facilitate the running of a modern 'glass cockpit', complete with multi-function displays, with high-speed/high-capacity computers, fly-by-wire flight controls and a head-up display (HUD). All these improvements would feature in the F-14D, for which Grumman received an $864 million contract in the summer of 1984.

Three years prior to this, in July 1981, the company had resumed flight operations with the original F-14B prototype that was now fitted with General Electric F101-DFE engines. Chosen by the USAF for its B-1B bomber and F-15 and F-16 fighters, the new engine (re-designated the F110 in October 1982) was capable of producing 27,000 lbs of thrust when installed in the F-14. The F110-GE-400 greatly enhanced

East Coast fleet replacement squadron VF-101 was the first frontline unit to receive the F-14A+ in early 1988, this squadron assuming training responsibility for both Atlantic and Pacific Fleet units slated for transition to the new aircraft. (US Navy)

Did you know?

An F-14A (BuNo 160666) from VF-111 notched up the Tomcat's one millionth flight hour in US Navy service on 26 March 1987. Its crew was the first to land and log, thus beating 25 other Tomcats that were airborne at that time to the record.

VF-211 'Fighting Checkmates' and sister-squadron VF-24 'Fighting Renegades' became the first Miramar-based units to be issued with the F-14A+ in the spring of 1989. However, their association with the aircraft was to be a brief one, as in 1992 they reverted back to the A-model when a paucity in the number of F-14Bs (as they were now designated) saw the US Navy decide to consolidate all remaining examples with Atlantic Fleet units. Seen shortly after its delivery to the 'Fighting Checkmates', this VF-211 jet is seen in 'Doomsday' configuration, toting six AIM-54Cs. (US Navy via Peter Mersky)

the Tomcat's mission performance thanks to its thrust levels being 32 percent higher than those of the TF30. Its lean fuel burn rate also boosted the jet's CAP loiter time by no less than 34 per cent. Being some 20 years younger than the Pratt & Whitney engine, the F110 was also designed from the outset to be far less susceptible to stalling at high angles of attack.

In February 1984 the Navy announced that it had instructed Grumman to install F110s in new production aircraft from 1988 onward. With engine testing complete by early 1987, Grumman duly commenced fitting F110s into airframes on the Calverton line. The first of 38 new-build F-14A+s was delivered to the NATC in November 1987, this aircraft featuring minor avionics and airframe changes as well. Perhaps the most significant of these was the installation of the new Direct Lift Control/Approach Power Control system, which made the Tomcat a much safer aircraft to fly when performing ACM or when 'low and slow' around the boat on recovery. The aircraft's radar warning receiver (RWR) equipment was also improved and its radar fire control system upgraded.

Aside from the new-build F-14A+s (re-designated F-14Bs in May 1991), a total of 47 F-14As were also returned to Grumman from the Fleet for upgrading. Following flight-testing at Patuxent River

'Although the F-14D programme was advertised as a threefold improvement in engines, avionics and radar, the hidden agenda was really to fix the engines at all costs.'
Rear Admiral Paul T Gillcrist

Did you know?
The F-14A+ was initially referred to as the Super Tomcat during the early stages of the F110 engine test programme.

and Point Mugu, the first examples were issued to VF-101 in 1988 – all units equipped with the F-14A+ were trained by this squadron.

By then, flight-testing of the F-14D was well underway, the prototype aircraft having completed its first hop from Calverton on 8 December 1987. Like the F-14A+, the D-model was powered by two F110-GE-400s that allowed the aircraft to launch from a carrier deck in dry power, rather than in fuel-draining reheat as had always been the case with the F-14A.

The airframe changes that came on line with the F-14A+ were also present in the D-model jet. However, the latter machine's avionics were appreciably different. At the heart of the improvements was the AN/APG-71 radar, which was broadly based on the AN/AWG-9 but with digital

processing and night vision goggles-capable displays. A development of the AN/APG-70 radar fitted in the USAF's F-15E Strike Eagle, the new system gave the F-14D improved detection and tracking range of aerial targets, thus allowing the jet to fire its AIM-54s at a greater distance from the contact. The D-model was also

The F-14D cockpits (front and back) merged the old with the new in a 'lashed-up lump-it-on-top' kind of way according to those that flew it. Multi-function displays sat rather uncomfortably alongside good old fashioned 'steam' gauges, and systems integration between the front and back seats was virtually non-existent. Such 'fire-walling' meant that there were certain systems that only the pilot could control and others that only the RIO could operate. (Danny Coremans/DACO)

equipped with a Mil-Std 1553 databus and dual AYK-14 computers, which helped run the jet's digitised cockpit and HUD, new RWR and improved secure communications equipment in the form of the Joint Tactical Information Distribution System. Externally, the aircraft boasted an AAS-42 Infrared Search and Track Set mounted in a distinctive dual chin pod alongside the AAX-1 Television Camera Set already that had been fitted as standard to all F-14A/Bs acquired by the US Navy (it was not fitted to Iranian jets, however).

The first production F-14D was delivered to the NATC in May 1990 and the second airframe sent to VX-4 at Point Mugu the following month. A total of 127 F-14Ds were originally scheduled for production, with a further 400+ A-models being upgraded to this standard by Grumman.

Tomcats from the Naval Air Warfare Center's Aircraft Division at Patuxent River prepare to run in over USS John C Stennis (CVN-74) and pitch out into the recovery pattern during the highly successful Digital Flight Control System trials staged off the Virginia coast in 1996. Leading the section is an F-14A, with a D-model jet in trail. (US Navy)

Following CVW-6's disestablishment on 1 April 1992, its two F-14 units (VF-11 'Red Rippers' and VF-31 'Tomcatters') were transferred to CVW-14 to replace the latter wing's VF-21 and VF-154, which had forward deployed to NAS Atsugi, Japan, to join CVW-5. Moving from Oceana to Miramar, VF-11 and VF-31 became the first fleet units to be equipped with the F-14D in early July 1992 following the completion of a three-month training syllabus with VF-124. 'Tomcatter 200' was VF-31's first D-model CAG jet, and it would ultimately receive high-visibility markings. This aircraft was lost in a midair collision with another F-14D from VF-31 off the California coast on 13 January 1995. (US Navy via Peter Mersky)

A F-14D from VF-11 closes up behind a USAF tanker during work-ups in 1994. This unit had to give up its D-model jets in 1997 due to a shortage of airframes, switching to the F-14B instead. (US Navy)

Did you know?
The F-14B/D could be catapulted from a carrier deck without the use of afterburner. Indeed, the pilot was restricted from using the latter because he could overspeed the catapult's launch gear, such was the thrust developed by the F110 engine when in afterburner.

However, with the end of the Cold War and the subsequent disbandment of 11 Fleet Tomcat squadrons, these production numbers were slashed by Congress to the point where just 59 F-14Ds were built – four converted test aircraft, 37 brand new jets and 18 A-model upgrades. The last new-build F-14D (and the last brand new Tomcat) was accepted by the US Navy on 10 July 1992.

On 2 August 1990 Iraqi forces invaded neighbouring Kuwait, catching the western world by surprise. When President George H W Bush announced the commencement of Operation *Desert Shield* four days later, the nearest American air power to the threatened Gulf states was USS *Independence* (CV-62), with VF-21 and VF-154 onboard as part of CVW-14. The purpose of *Desert Shield* was to deter Iraqi leader President Saddam Hussein from ordering his victorious army into Saudi Arabia. USS *Dwight D Eisenhower* (CVN-69) bolstered the US naval presence in the region on 8 August when it steamed from the eastern Mediterranean through the Suez Canal into the Red Sea. Its embarked air wing – CVW-7 – included VF-142 and

◄

VF-143 'Pukin' Dogs' was one of four Tomcat squadrons that provided protection for vulnerable Gulf states in the immediate aftermath of the Iraqi invasion of Kuwait in August 1990. Operation Desert Shield *saw F-14A+ equipped VF-142 and VF-143 flying fully armed jets on standing patrols over Saudi Arabia from their carrier, CVN-69, which was sailing in the Red Sea. Both units were giving the F-14A+ its fleet debut during this particular cruise. (US Navy)*

CVW-1, embarked in USS America (CV-66), was one of the most active air wings in Desert Storm. Initially operating from the Red Sea, along with the rest of the Atlantic Fleet carriers involved in the campaign, it subsequently sailed into the NAG in early February so as to directly support the retaking of Kuwait by Coalition ground forces. This photograph was taken in late January 1991, when CVW-1's two Tomcat units (VF-33 'Starfighters', seen here, and VF-102 'Diamondbacks') were providing escorts and MiGCAPs for the Hornets and Intruders from the air wing sent to attack targets in Kuwait and Iraq. (US Navy via Peter Mersky)

VF-143, which were giving the F-14A+ its operational debut.

By the time these two vessels were replaced in-theatre by five carriers hastily despatched from the USA and one from Japan (without any Tomcats embarked), more than 500,000 American and Coalition troops had been committed to *Desert Shield*. Despite this overwhelming force massing on the borders of Iraq and Kuwait, Saddam Hussein refused to withdraw his troops from the latter country and Operation *Desert Storm* was launched on 17 January 1991.

Some 99 Tomcats would see action during this one-sided conflict, with the F-14As of VF-14 and VF-32 embarked in USS *John F Kennedy* (CV-67), the F-14A+s of VF-74 and VF-103 aboard USS *Saratoga* (CV-60) and the F-14As from VF-33 and VF-102 aboard USS *America* (CV-66) all operating from the Red Sea. The latter carrier moved into the NAG in early February prior to the start of the ground war. USS *Ranger* (CV-61), with the F-14As of VF-1 and VF-2 on board, and USS *Theodore Roosevelt* (CVN-71), with the F-14As of VF-41 and VF-84 embarked, had been operating in the NAG from the start of the conflict.

Once CV-66 had taken up station in the NAG, VF-33 switched from flying strike escorts and MiGCAPs to the far more mundane fleet air defence role. This aircraft was photographed flying just such a sortie in late February 1991. (US Navy via Peter Mersky)

'There was lot of parochialism as to where the F-14 and F-15 fighter CAPs were placed. The Eagles got the kills because it was the USAF's E-3 AWACS that were running the show up north. They would even call Navy guys off and then bring in Eagles for easy pickings. This could just be the ranting and raving of pissed-off Navy pilots, but from what I personally saw in Operation *Desert Storm*, there was probably a shred of truth in these stories.'

Lt Doug Denneny, VF-14
USS *John F Kennedy* (CV-67)

Did you know?

Most CAP missions flown by the Tomcat during *Desert Storm* lasted five to seven hours with inflight refuelling, whilst most strike escort sorties averaged just three hours in duration.

Tomcat units would fly mainly strike escort and TARPS missions during the war. The high hopes that the fighter community had of adding to the jet's victory haul were stymied by the IrAF's non-appearance in its patrol sectors. Up until the invasion of Kuwait, when the F-14 units were allocated a single CAP station over Iraq, the Tomcats had been tasked with performing defensive CAPs for the carrier battlegroups in the Red Sea and the NAG. When the jets did venture over enemy territory whilst escorting strike

VF-1's sister-squadron VF-2 was also kept busy flying strike escorts, MiGCAPs and fleet air defence missions, as well as carrying out the vital TARPS role. Indeed, the 'Bounty Hunters' flew more than 500 combat missions and 1900 flying hours during the 43 days of Desert Storm – more than any other tactical squadron operating in-theatre. (Pete Clayton)

mission, the IrAF refused to engage them. Some Naval Aviators felt that the Iraqi pilots chose to flee whenever they picked up emissions from the F-14s' AN/AWG-9 radar. There was also a feeling within the Tomcat community that USAF E-3 AWACS controllers who ran the interceptions of IrAF aircraft favoured the allocation of F-15Cs to deal with the enemy threat.

In reality, Tomcats had been kept out of the aerial action because the US Navy had failed to develop the necessary systems –

F-14As from VF-1 and VF-2 enjoy some rare down time between sorties in January 1991. Crews have already strapped themselves into the two 'Wolfpack' jets furthest from the camera, however, so they will be launching shortly. The fairing covering the extendable refuelling probe was removed by most Tomcat units involved in Desert Storm so as to prevent it getting snagged in the refuelling baskets deployed behind USAF and RAF big wing tankers in-theatre. Should a fairing have been ripped off, it could easily have disappeared down the right engine intake and caused the Tomcat to crash. (Pete Clayton)

primarily up-to-date Identification Friend of Foe (IFF) equipment – and procedures required to integrate carrier air wings as part of a joint air component command. This meant that F-14 crews were unable to solve the strict Rules of Engagement (RoE) that would have allowed them to autonomously engage aerial targets using only their onboard sensors. Instead, they had to rely on controlling platforms such as USAF E-3s to give them their clearance to fire.

Lt Stuart Broce and Lt Cdr Ron McElraft used this jet (BuNo 162603) to achieve the only aerial victory credited to the F-14 in Desert Storm when they used an AIM-9M to down a Mil Mi-8 helicopter on 6 February 1991 – this kill marking was added to the jet upon its return to CV-61. The aircraft was subsequently lost on 23 June 2000 while flying from CVN-74 off Hawaii when it suffered a cold catapult shot. Both crewmen ejected and were rescued. (US Navy)

'It was obvious that the Iraqis did not want to fight, and they were running from us, or we were shooting them out of the sky. They wouldn't go anywhere near an F-14. That's a big part of the reason why the F-14s didn't get any kills against fixed wing aircraft.'

Lt Cdr Dave Parsons, VF-32
USS *John F Kennedy* (CV-67)

With the RoE criteria met, fighters with Beyond Visual Range air-to-air missiles like the AIM-7 Sparrow and AIM-54 Phoenix could fire their ordnance at long range, safe in the knowledge that no friendly aircraft in the area would be shot down instead. USAF F-15C pilots could solve all the required RoE criteria for identifying an enemy aircraft from within their own cockpits, prior to shooting it down. The F-14, conversely, lacked the IFF systems and software to meet all RoE criteria, which left its crew reliant on outside clearance to engage. The job of defeating the IrAF was therefore given to the Eagle pilots, who duly shot down 35 aircraft.

Ultimately, the F-14 performed just six intercepts resulting in a solitary aerial kill in *Desert Storm*. The latter took the form of a Mil Mi-8 helicopter that was shot down by a crew from VF-1 on 6 February 1991. This victory went some way to evening up for the score for the Tomcat, as VF-103 had lost a jet to an SA-2 SAM on 21 January – its pilot had been rescued and the radar intercept officer (RIO) captured. This aircraft had been flying a TARPS mission, proving that these sorties were usually more action packed than the traditional fighter missions flown by the Tomcat in *Desert Storm*.

damage assessment photographs in the wake of air strikes by carrier-based attack aircraft. TARPS-equipped F-14s also helped in the daily hunt for Iraq's mobile 'Scud' ballistic missiles.

Despite maintaining a mission capable rate of 77 per cent, logging a total of 4,182 sorties and completing 14,248 flight hours (more than all other US Navy fixed-wing aircraft) during the 43-day air war, the F-14 had proven largely ineffective in its primary role as an interceptor. And at this point in the jet's history, being a fighter was still virtually the only role it could perform. This would all change in the early 1990s with the advent of the multi-role 'Bombcat'.

The importance of the tactical reconnaissance mission grew as the conflict progressed, for the US Navy had quickly found that it could not rely on USAF tactical reconnaissance assets for up-to-date bomb

'Big wing' tanker support was critical to the success of Desert Storm. Proving the point, an F-14A+ from VF-103 'Clubbers' is seen taking on fuel from an Ohio Air National Guard KC-135E over the Red Sea in February 1991. This photograph was taken from a TARPS pod slung beneath a second Tomcat from the unit. The 'Clubbers' lost a TARPS configured jet to an SA-2 SAM over Iraq on 21 January 1991 – this was the only US Navy Tomcat ever lost to enemy action. (US Navy via Peter Mersky)

'BOMBCAT'

The post-*Desert Storm* years were bleak ones for the US Navy's fighter community, with swingeing budget cuts seeing 11 Fleet Tomcat units decommissioned due to the aircraft's astronomical maintenance costs and single-mission capability. However, just when it looked like the F-14's ocean-going days were numbered, a reprieve came thanks to the accelerated demise of another Grumman 'Ironworks' product. The all-weather long-range A-6 Intruder bomber was hastily chopped again due to high maintenance costs and the supposed evaporation of its mission in the post-Cold War world.

With the Intruder on the verge of retirement, and the Tomcat seemingly following in its footsteps, the US Navy now found itself facing a shortage of tactical carrier aircraft to fulfil its global 'policing' mission. When the F-14 was developed

in the late 1960s, Grumman had built the jet with the capability to drop bombs, although this mission requirement had not been specified by the US Navy.

For the first two decades of its service life, the Tomcat had been operated exclusively as a fighter, with the additional photo-reconnaissance role being adopted begrudgingly by fleet squadrons in the

'The Tomcat's distinct size and power made it an intimidating foe to any enemy. With the big motors in the F-14B/D, its speed and power were very impressive. Coupled with size, large ordnance load and long legs, the Tomcat could really reach out and touch the bad guys in Operation *Southern Watch*.'

Cdr Will Cooney, commanding officer of VF-32
USS *Harry S Truman* (CVN-75)

The Naval Air Test Center's NF-14A 'Salty Dog 202' releases a GBU-24 LGB at supersonic speeds over the test range at Patuxent River. Note that the aircraft is covered in photo-calibration discs and is carrying test cameras in its modified external tanks. This jet was heavily utilised during the 'Bombcat' development programme undertaken at 'Pax River' in 1990. (US Navy)

early 1980s. Indeed, there was a bumper sticker popular in the fighter community at Miramar and Oceana throughout this time that bore the mantra 'Not a pound for air-to-ground', referring to the fact that the F-14 was an interceptor through and through. However, once threatened with wholesale decommissioning in the post-Cold War 1990s, the Tomcat units looked to

diversify in order to survive. Seeing that the precision bombing role once performed by the A-6 was now vacant, a push was made to pair the F-14 up with some form of bolt-on targeting pod system.

Experimentation with gravity bombs hung beneath standard Tomcats had taken place just prior to *Desert Storm*, although senior naval officers realised that the

F-14 would not be a viable fighter/attack platform without some kind of precision weapons delivery capability. Little funding was available to develop such a system, so an 'off-the-shelf' pod was acquired thanks to the securing of modest financing through the lobbying of Commander Naval Air Forces Atlantic in the autumn of 1994. The equipment chosen was the combat-proven AN/AAQ-14 LANTIRN (low-altitude navigation and targeting infra-red night)

pod, developed for the F-15E by Martin Marietta (later Lockheed Martin).

Working with a tiny budget, the Tomcat community, ably assisted by a clutch of defence contractors, integrated the digital pod with the analogue F-14A/B, and by March 1995 a test aircraft – supplied by VF-103 – was dropping laser-guided bombs (LGBs) with the aid of the AN/AAQ-25 LANTIRN (as the US Navy designated the modified AN/AAQ-14). The results of this early evaluation were stunning, with the Tomcat crew obtaining better infra-red imagery, and bomb accuracy, than the similarly-equipped USAF F-15E Strike Eagle and F-16C Fighting Falcon. On 14 June 1996 the first fleet-capable LANTIRN pod was delivered to VF-103 at NAS Oceana. During the ceremony held to mark this occasion, Secretary of the Navy John H

Dalton proudly proclaimed 'The Cat is back'.

To give an unsophisticated bomber like the basic F-14 a precision targeting capability, the basic LANTIRN system was modified into US Navy-specific LTS (LANTIRN Targeting System) configuration. Martin Marietta removed the navigation pod of the two-pod LANTIRN system and vastly improved the targeting pod for Tomcat use. The US Navy pod featured an embedded GPS and inertial measurement unit that provided it with line-of-site cueing and weapon release ballistics. The RIO had a much larger display in his cockpit than the one presented to his equivalent Weapon Systems Officer in the F-15E, which led to better apparent magnification and target recognition.

Unlike its USAF configurations, the LTS performed all the weapon release calculations and presented release cues

that it had generated to the aircrew. It also incorporated a masking avoidance curve display and, eventually, a north orientation cue and 40,000 ft-capable laser. The latter would prove extremely useful in allowing F-14 aircrew to employ LGBs above potential threat system altitudes especially in the higher terrain of Afghanistan during Operation *Enduring Freedom* (OEF).

But all that lay in the future, for in June 1996 the F-14/LTS partnership remained

VF-211 was the first Pacific Fleet Tomcat unit to complete the Advanced Attack Readiness Program in June 1992, which gave crews exposure to the same kind of ground attack training undertaken by Naval Aviators flying the A-6 Intruder and F/A-18 Hornet. This F-14A, armed with four 500-lb Mk 82 bombs, was photographed commencing its attack run on the range at MCAS Twenty Nine Palms, California, in July 1996. This base is home to the Marine Air Ground Task Force Training Command and Combat Center. (US Navy)

in USS *Nimitz* (CVN-68), dropped LGBs (designated by F/A-18s) on an ammunition dump in eastern Bosnia.

Aside from brief campaigns in the Balkans (1995 and 1999) and Afghanistan (2001–02), combat operations for F-14 pilots and naval flight officers during the jet's final 15 years of frontline service had taken place from carriers sailing in the NAG. In the wake of *Desert Storm*, a No-Fly Zone had been created over southern Iraq – with UN backing – as Operation *Southern Watch* (OSW) on 26 August 1992 in order to protect Shi'ite Muslims from persecution by Saddam Hussein's regime. Joint Task Force-Southwest Asia (JTF-SWA), consisting of units from the United States, Britain, France and Saudi Arabia, was established on the same date to oversee the day-to-day running of OSW.

unproven in combat. Nine months earlier, in a precursor of things to come, the Tomcat briefly had the chance to prove its worth in the 'mud moving' business when, on 5 September 1995 during Operation *Allied Force*, two F-14As from VF-41, embarked

The Tomcat proved to be a primary asset in OSW, although not because of its ability as a long-range fighter. As had been the case in *Desert Storm*, the F-14's TARPS capability provided JTF-SWA with the flexibility to monitor Iraqi military activity on a daily basis in good weather. Although the TARPS mission was seen as a necessary evil by a number of dyed-in-the-wool fighter crews, it nevertheless enabled the Tomcat community to make a concrete contribution to the daily enforcing of OSW. TARPS sorties also tended to be far more eventful than the typically mundane and boring CAPs that were the 'bread and butter' sorties of the F-14 units in-theatre in the years prior to the arrival of LTS-equipped aircraft.

The ultimate F-14 bomber toting a LANTIRN pod had to wait until 16 December 1998 to prove its worth in OSW. On that

date the US Navy spearheaded Operation *Desert Fox* in what proved to be a precursor for Operation *Iraqi Freedom* five years later. F-14Bs from VF-32 were involved in the first wave of attacks against Iraqi air defence installations, dropping self-guided GBU-12, GBU-16 and GBU-24 LGBs. The Tomcats also 'lased' for accompanying F/A-18 Hornets. Two days later the F-14Ds of VF-213 joined in the action from USS *Carl Vinson* (CVN-70).

A section of F-14Bs from VF-102 head north to Kuwait from USS George Washington (CVN-73) at the start of a laser-bombing training mission in February 1998. Each aircraft carries Laser-Guided Training Rounds on Triple Ejector Racks attached to the forward underfuselage pallets. (US Navy)

> Tomcats would occasionally carry out sea surveillance during their patrols in the NAG. This F-14D from VF-31, embarked in USS Abraham Lincoln (CVN-72) in August 1998, is armed with an AIM-54C and a rarely seen Mk 7 cluster munitions dispenser. (Lt Jim Muse)

> A crewman from VF-32 paints bomb tally symbols on an F-14B in a lull between airstrikes against Iraq during Operation Desert Fox. By the time the four-day offensive against Iraqi targets had ended, the F-14 had proven itself to be the precision bomber of choice in the region. (US Navy)

During the four days of *Desert Fox*, VF-32 alone had dropped 111,054 lbs of ordnance, consisting of 16 GBU-10s, 16 GBU-16s and no fewer than 26 2,000-lb GBU-24 penetrator LGBs. The latter proved to be the laser-guided weapon of choice against hardened aircraft shelters, HQ bunkers and command & control buildings. Not all of the Tomcats sortied were carrying bombs, however, as both VF-32 and VF-213 also conducted a series of escort CAPs for USAF B-1Bs committed to *Desert Fox* from day two of the campaign.

The adoption of a more aggressive stance by the IrAF after this campaign almost resulted in a US Navy Tomcat claiming its first Phoenix missile kill when, on 5 January 1999, two F-14Ds from VF-213 fired two AIM-54Cs at MiG-25s that had penetrated the No-Fly Zone. The Iraqi jets

Assigned to CVW-8, VF-14 and VF-41 were committed to Operation Deliberate Force *in March 1999. Flying F-14As the units expended close to 800,000 lbs of LGBs and iron bombs. F-14A 'Tophatter 100' is armed with two 500lb Mk 82 iron bombs and live AIM-7Ms and AIM-9Ms. (US Navy)*

had already turned back north and were making a high-speed run for home by the time the Tomcats got to fire their missiles at very long range. Neither hit their intended targets.

Two months later, in March, the Tomcat returned to action over the Balkans when VF-14 and VF-41 were committed to Operation *Deliberate Force* – NATO's campaign to free Kosovo from Serbian control. Flying venerable F-14As from the USS *Theodore Roosevelt* (CVN-71), the units expended close to 800,000 lbs of LGBs and iron bombs. Crews from both squadrons also functioned as Forward Air Controllers (Airborne) for other assets involved in the Kosovo campaign. VF-14 CO, Cdr Ted Carter, explained how the FAC(A) mission was carried out:

We flew in sections, one aircraft serving as an escort for the other. Each F-14

The CVW-8 Tomcats involved in Allied Force typically carried four bombs apiece (here, two 1,000 lb GBU-16s on the starboard pallet and a pair of 500 lb GBU-12s to port), which could be used for both striking a target or for marking an aim point for other fighter-bomber aircraft being controlled by the Tomcat crew. VF-14 and VF-41 perfected the Forward Air Controllers (Airborne) role for the Tomcat community in combat conditions during the Kosovo campaign. (US Navy)

'It is perhaps the ultimate irony that the Tomcat, designed to be the supreme air superiority machine, left a much larger combat legacy as a precision strike fighter – a role it was never meant to perform.'

Lt Cdr Dave Parsons

usually carried four bombs, which we used for both striking a target ourselves or for marking a target for other strike aircraft. The FAC(A) is like a quarterback on a football team, seeking out and identifying targets, ushering strike aircraft to the scene, recommending the type of ordnance for a particular target, ensuring they recognised potential terrain hazards, and providing them with run-in and recovery headings.

Units committed to carrying out the OSW mission continued to counter Iraqi AAA and SAM opposition during 1999, and on 9 September, following a heightened response to its patrols, CVW-2, embarked in USS *Constellation* (CV-64), launched Operation *Gun Smoke*. Some 35 of 39 AAA and SAM sites targeted for destruction were eliminated in a series of precision strikes that saw the largest expenditure of ordnance in a single day since *Desert Storm*.

On 9 September 1999, CVW-2, embarked in CV-64, launched a one-day series of intensive strikes on AAA and SAM sites in southern Iraq as part of Operation Gun Smoke. F-14D equipped VF-2 was in the vanguard of the campaign, and one of its crews also got to fire off a single AIM-54C against an Iraqi MiG-23. As with the VF-213 Phoenix incident nine months earlier, the shot was taken at extreme range and the weapon missed its target. (Cdr Tom Twomey)

During the first nine months of 1999, US and British aircraft flew 10,000 OSW sorties and dropped 1,000 bombs on 400 targets in Iraq. This level of action was sustained into the new millennium, and between March 2000 and March 2001, Coalition aircraft were engaged more than 500 times by SAMs and AAA while flying a further 10,000 sorties into Iraqi airspace. Amongst the units to spar with Iraq's ground-to-air defences during the latter half of 2000 was VF-103 'Jolly Rogers', embarked in CVN-73. These F-14Bs are seen chained down to the stern of 'GW' ready to launch on their next OSW patrol. Note the bomb tally on the nose of the unit's colour jet. (US Navy)

VF-32 flew yet more LGB strikes against Iraqi command, control and communications sites in February 2001 during CVW-3's debut cruise aboard the then new Nimitz class carrier USS Harry S Truman (CVN-75). It also undertook vital TARPS missions and conducted Defensive Counter-Air (DCA) sweeps in the OSW patrol area. (US Navy)

The F-14Ds of VF-2 played a leading part in the success of this campaign, and aside from dropping LGBs, the unit also got to fire a single AIM-54C against an Iraqi MiG-23 – again without success.

Tensions remained high over Iraq well into 2001, and on 16 February CVW-3, operating from USS *Harry S Truman* (CVN-75), targeted five command, control and communications sites. Again, VF-32 found itself in the vanguard of the one-day war, dropping LGBs, lasing for fellow Hornet strikers, running TARPS missions and conducting Defensive Counter Air sweeps in the OSW patrol area.

The steady escalation of the conflict in the region was only brought to a halt, albeit temporarily, by the devastating attacks on the World Trade Center, in New York City, and the Pentagon on 11 September 2001. The subsequent declaration of the War on Terror by President George W Bush saw US carrier battle groups under Fifth Fleet control removed from their OSW station and pushed further east into the Arabian Sea and Indian Ocean in order to support Operation *Enduring Freedom* in Afghanistan.

Now a truly multi-role fighter-bomber, with more mission taskings than any other aircraft then embarked in a US carrier, the venerable Tomcat was set to play a leading role in the conflicts over Afghanistan and Iraq, rather than being the bit-part player that is had been in *Desert Storm*.

The first operations conducted by the F-14 during the final phase of its operational life occurred just hours after the 'twin towers' and the Pentagon had been attacked by al-Qaeda terrorists in hijacked airliners. That morning, VF-11 and VF-143 were preparing to embark in CV-67 as part of CVW-7's cruise work-ups off the Virginia coast. North American Aerospace Defense Command (NORAD) contacted the US Navy soon after the south tower was hit and asked for its help in securing the airspace over the eastern seaboard. Both CV-67 and CVN-73 were put to sea by Second Fleet, and the vessels embarked a handful of fighter squadrons from NAS Oceana.

VF-11 and VF-143 were sent to CV-67, and pilot Lt(jg) Joseph Greentree from the latter unit subsequently flew several missions in support of the NORAD-controlled sea shield that had been hastily established off the coast of New York;

For the first 72 hours that VF-11 and VF-143 were embarked in *Kennedy*, we flew round-the-clock CAPs up and down the eastern seaboard. The skies remained eerily empty during this time, with all civilian air traffic having been grounded. After three days Second Fleet told us to abandon these CAP missions and commence our work-ups.

With al-Qaeda directly linked to the 11 September attacks, the US government turned its attention to the terrorist group's home in Afghanistan. Less than three weeks after the atrocities in New York City and Washington, DC, carrier-based aircraft would be in the vanguard of a

Did you know?
Tomcat groundcrew were spending 50 hours maintaining the jet for every hour that it flew during the final decade of its service. This figure compared to 5-10 hours per flight hour for its replacement, the F/A-18E/F.

joint operation to remove the Taleban from power and destroy the organisational infrastructure that al-Qaeda had established in Afghanistan.

The carrier closest to this land-locked country was USS *Enterprise* (CVN-65), with the F-14As of VF-14 and VF-41 embarked. These units were nearing the

end of their last cruise with the Tomcat, and had seen action in Iraq during five weeks of OSW patrols. Also steaming towards the Arabian Sea from the Indian Ocean was USS *Carl Vinson* (CVN-70), with the F-14Ds of VF-213 embarked. These three Tomcat units would be in the vanguard of what was codenamed Operation

Congestion on the tanker was a common problem facing Tomcat crews returning from long-range strikes short on fuel during OEF. This photograph was taken during 'front side' refuelling, however, when fuel was not so critical for F-14 crews as they headed into Afghanistan. Getting on the tanker expeditiously was always an issue for pilots flying the notoriously short-legged Hornet. Here, watched by an F-14D from VF-213, a section of F/A-18Cs from VFA-94 'Mighty Shrikes' take it in turns to top off their tanks from a Diego Garcia-based KC-10A assigned to the 32nd Aerial Refueling Squadron/305th Air Mobility Wing. (Lt Tony Toma)

Enduring Freedom (OEF) by Pentagon planners.

Sailing off the coast of Pakistan in the Northern Arabian Sea, both carriers were in position to commence strikes on al-Qaeda and Taleban targets by late September, although the first OEF mission was not generated until 8 October 2001. Politically prevented from using nearby land bases

in the NAG and India, and unwilling to over-use frontline airfields in Pakistan, Uzbekistan and Tajikistan, aircraft carriers were the only way initially open to the US military to bring tactical air power to bear in Afghanistan. The strike fighters of CVW-8 (CVN-65) and CVW-11 (CVN-70) duly hit terrorist training camps, Taleban barracks, air bases and SAM/AAA sites in the longest carrier-launched strikes in history. Tomcat, Hornet and Prowler units routinely operated more than 700 miles (1,126 km) from their carriers in sorties that lasted between six and ten hours.

With no Coalition troops in-theatre to support during the early phase of OEF, the Tomcat crews worked instead with two-man Special Operations Forces (SOF) teams, who sought out targets for the Naval Aviators to attack – they would

CAPT David "Merc" Mercer
DCAG
CAPT Jack "Yukon" Godl
CAG

With their OEF mission over, VF-14's Lt Cdr Van Kizer and his RIO Lt Dave Bailey keep their hands in the air, and away from the weapons activation panel, while armourers pin the pylon firing mechanisms for the ordnance attached to 'Tophatter 200'. A 40-mission veteran of Operation Allied Force *in 1999, Lt Cdr Kizer would fly a further 20 sorties in OEF. (VF-14)*

also provide crews with target 'talk-ons'. Thanks to the F-14's legendary range, the jet was also tasked with taking out targets in the far north and west of Afghanistan. US Navy strike aircraft relied heavily on 'big wing' tanker support throughout

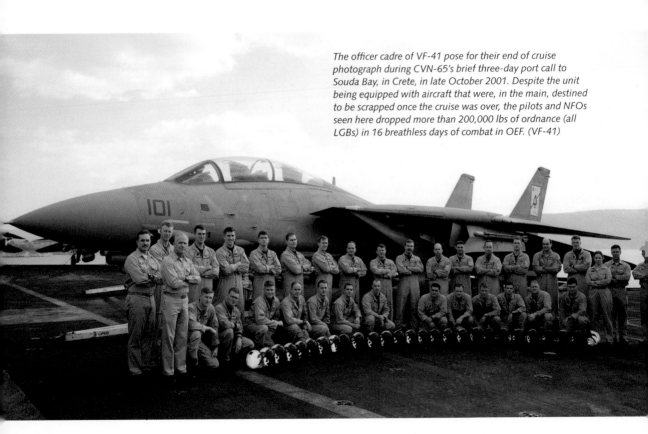

The officer cadre of VF-41 pose for their end of cruise photograph during CVN-65's brief three-day port call to Souda Bay, in Crete, in late October 2001. Despite the unit being equipped with aircraft that were, in the main, destined to be scrapped once the cruise was over, the pilots and NFOs seen here dropped more than 200,000 lbs of ordnance (all LGBs) in 16 breathless days of combat in OEF. (VF-41)

OEF, with crews refuelling at least three times from KC-10s, KC-135s, VC10Ks and Tristars during the course of these marathon missions.

Exclusively employing LGBs, VF-14 and VF-41 expended some 380,000 lbs of ordnance between 8 and 23 October, when CVN-65 was relieved by CVN-71 (with the F-14Bs of VF-102 embarked). 'VF-41 achieved an 82 per cent hit rate, which was a level of accuracy that had never previously been achieved by the US Navy', recalled squadron CO, Cdr Brian Gawne. Both Tomcat squadrons in CVW-8 also buddy-lased Maverick missiles and LGBs for Hornet units.

VF-213 was in the thick of the action during this period as well, with the unit being heavily involved in supporting the Northern Alliance's ground offensive against the Taleban in November. On the 5th of that month, the squadron's CO, Cdr Chip King, and his NFO, Lt Cdr Michael Peterson, made history when they became the first US Navy crew to use the F-14's 20 mm cannon in action. King recalled, 'I remember thinking to myself at the time what a disparity in technology. It was like "Buck Rogers" meeting the "Arabian Nights", as the Taleban fighters that we were strafing were on horseback'.

Both VF-213 and VF-102 flew some of the most challenging missions of OEF as Taleban and al-Qaeda fighters fled east towards the Tora Bora cave complex and the Pakistani border. CVN-70 was eventually relieved by USS *John C Stennis* (CVN-74) on 15 December 2001, by which time VF-213 had expended 452 LGBs and 470 20 mm cannon rounds.

➤ *VF-213 CO Cdr Chip King (left) and Lt Cdr Kevin Claffy compare notes on the flightdeck of CVN-70 at the end of an OEF mission flown on 28 October 2001. Behind them, one of VF-213's hard-working armourer teams has already started uploading GBU-12 LGBs onto the jet's belly pallet rails. (Lt Tony Toma)*

➤➤ *Armed with a pair of 1,000-lb GBU-16 LGBs, VF-213's 'Blacklion 101' closes on a KC-10 for front side gas during an OEF mission. The 'Black Lions' expended 157 GBU-16s during the OEF campaign. Bomb loadouts were constantly altered as the war progressed due to the changing nature of the targets on the ground. (USAF)*

The F-14As of VF-211 were embarked in CVN-74, and four days after the unit's arrival in-theatre the Tora Bora offensive ended and the fighting in Afghanistan drastically reduced in its intensity. Things did not flare up again until early March 2002, when the US Army's Task Force Mountain launched Operation *Anaconda* in the mountains of eastern Afghanistan. Targeting 1,000+ hardcore al-Qaeda fighters entrenched in ridgelines and caves throughout the Shar-i-Kot Valley, the offensive got badly bogged

down to the point where the survival of US troops in contact with the enemy was only ensured through the overwhelming employment of tactical air power.

During the final stages of *Anaconda* CVN-71 was finally relieved by CV-67, whose CVW-7 (including VF-11 and VF-143) flew its first missions on 11 March.

An F-14B from VF-11 made history on this date when its crew dropped the first Joint Direct Attack Munition (JDAM) expended in combat by a Tomcat. This

VF-211's 'Nickel 104' (BuNo 158618) accelerates down CVN-74's waist cat four in Zone Five afterburner during an early Operation Anaconda mission. This aircraft was lost on 8 March 2002 when its tailhook separated on landing at the completion of an OEF mission. Both crewmen successfully ejected. Delivered to the US Navy in October 1972, it had spent many years in the Tomcat test programme with VX-4, before being refurbished in the early 1980s. (US Navy)

GPS-guided weapon would subsequently see use with F-14B/D-equipped units (the A-model lacked the software to employ JDAM) in OIF.

In the autumn of 2002, the focus of the War on Terror switched to Iraq. By then the Tomcat had proven itself to be a true multi-role combat platform capable of precision bombing, buddy laser target designation through use of the LTS pod, FAC(A), Strike Co-ordinating Armed Reconnaissance (SCAR), photo and digital reconnaissance

and, of course, fighter interception. One of the primary weapons that would be employed by the Tomcat in OIF was the GBU-31 2,000-lb JDAM. Initially cleared for use by the F-14B only, the JDAM was hastily made compatible with the F-14D through the installation of the D04 weapons computer upgrade in the weeks leading up to OIF. VF-2, embarked with CVW-2 in USS Constellation (CV-64), was the first D-model unit to get the upgrade.

On 28 February 2003, the unit dropped

➤ VF-11's Lt Cdr Chris Chope and his pilot take on mid-mission fuel in their F-14B from a USAF KC-10 during an OEF patrol in May 2002. (Lt Cdr Chris Chope)

➤➤ 'Ordies' from VF-103 load 20 mm cannon rounds into the magazine of an F-14B on the deck of CVN-73. A gun jam on 20 July 2002 ruined VF-103's one and only chance to see combat in OEF. Strafing Taleban and al-Qaeda fighters has become more commonplace of late in Afghanistan, as fast jet crews have little surface-to-air threat to be concerned about in-theatre. (US Navy)

VF-103's CAG jet returns to CVN-73 with its two GBU-12s still in place. Assigned to VF-102 in 1988, this aircraft joined VF-103 in 2000 and completed three combat tours with the squadron. The Tomcat was retired to Davis-Monthan AFB on 5 January 2005. (Capt Dana Potts)

Configured as a TARPS jet in the opening stages of OIF, VF-31's 'Tomcatter 101' was restricted to DCA patrols until fitted with an LTS pod as the ground war got into full swing. Seen returning from a TARPS mission soon after 'A-Day' (21 March 2003), the jet has just topped off its tanks from KC-135R 62-3505. (Lt Jim Muse)

Armed with two AIM-9Ms and an AIM-54C, VF-2's F-14D BuNo 159613 takes on fuel from a KC-10 during a pre-war DCA patrol in the OSW 'Box' over southern Iraq in late February 2003. CVW-2 relied heavily on tanker support in both OSW and OIF. (US Navy)

VF-2's 'Bullet 104' makes a heavy landing back aboard CV-64 in the NAG in mid-April 2003, shortly after hostilities has ended in OIF I. The Tomcat's robust undercarriage had been specially engineered by Grumman to cope with rough treatment such as this during 'blue water' ops. (US Navy)

the first GBU-31s expended by an F-14D in anger during an OSW mission over southern Iraq. The D-model Tomcats of VF-31 aboard USS *Abraham Lincoln* (CVN-72) were reconfigured with D04 straight after VF-2.

Assigned to CVW-14, VF-31 had been on deployment with the air wing since 20 July 2002. The final Tomcat unit to receive the D04 mission tape upgrade was VF-213, operating from USS *Theodore Roosevelt* (CVN-71) in the Mediterranean Sea.

Of the two remaining Tomcat squadrons committed to the conflict, VF-32, again in the Mediterranean aboard USS *Harry S Truman* (CVN-74), had had its F-14Bs made JDAM-compatible prior to deployment, but VF-154's baseline A-models, flying from USS *Kitty Hawk* (CV-63) in the NAG, remained restricted to LGBs. VF-2 was at

the forefront of OIF from the word go, participating in the 'Shock and Awe' strikes on Baghdad on the night of 21-22 March 2003. Indeed, CVW-2 provided the lead Coalition strike force to hit targets in the Iraqi capital, its Tomcats dropping JDAM as well as performing defensive counter air and reconnaissance missions for CVW-2. Operating from Fifth Fleet's designated OIF night carrier, VF-2 proceeded to fly the bulk of its missions masked by the cover of darkness. It initially used JDAM to hit fixed targets such as command and control nodes, SAM and radar sites, airfields and Republican Guard barracks, as well as presidential palaces and Ba'ath party buildings.

The Tomcat squadron then switched to CAS strikes as the push towards Baghdad gained momentum. The Tomcat's ability to

Proudly displaying its bomb tally, VF-2's 'Bullet 106' (BuNo 164342) taxis towards one of CV-64's bow catapults on 15 April 2003. The carrier departed the NAG for home 48 hours later. (US Navy)

Laden down with four GBU-12s, VF-154 'Black Knights' 'Nite 103' takes flight after being shot off one of CV-63's waist catapults to signal the start of yet another OIF mission. The jet would return to the carrier three hours later minus its LGBs. (US Navy)

> A Naval Aviator from VF-154 checks the guidance vanes on a 2000-lb GBU-24 Paveway III LGB. The weapon's large stabilisation package allows it to travel farther in flight. The unit expended 358 LGBs between 21 March and 14 April 2003, flying primarily FAC(A) and SCAR missions. (US Navy)

> A division of four Qatar det F-14As prepare to taxi out for a dusk mission at Al Udeid in April 2003. Behind them are F-16CJs from the USAF's 389th FS, RAAF F/A-18As from No 75 Sqn and RAF Tornado GR 4s. The VF-154 crews worked closely with all three types. (VF-154)

perform the demanding FAC(A) and SCAR roles for other strike fighter assets was also greatly appreciated as Coalition forces engaged the Republican Guard around cities such as Karbala and An Nasiriyah.

During the 28 days of OIF, VF-2 successfully completed 195 combat sorties totalling 887.5 hours. Its ten aircraft dropped 221 LGBs (217 GBU-12s and 4 GBU-16s) and 61 GBU-31 JDAM. Some 1,704 20 mm cannon rounds were also fired in strafing passes and no fewer than 125 targets were photographed using TARPS.

The other Tomcat squadrons in the NAG also flew a broad mix of missions ranging from precision strikes to CAS and FAC(A). VF-31 was flying from CVN-72, which was the designated day carrier. The unit operated closely with VFA-115, which was

conducting the very first cruise with the F/A-18E Super Hornet as part of CVW-14. With the latter jet boasting Tomcat-like endurance, VF-31 often flew mixed section strike missions with VFA-115.

By the time CVN-72 and CVW-14 were relieved in-theatre by USS *Nimitz* (CVN-68) and CVW-11 (which was the first air wing to deploy with Super Hornets rather than Tomcats) on 14 April, VF-31 had flown an astounding 585 combat sorties totalling 1,744 combat hours during its ten-month OEF/OSW/OIF deployment. The unit had delivered 56 JDAM, 165 GBU-12s, five GBU-16s, 13 Mk 82 'dumb' bombs and 1,355 20 mm cannon rounds.

Unable to employ JDAM with its F-14As, VF-154's war was undoubtedly the most unusual of any of the Tomcat units committed to OIF. Deployed on its final cruise with the F-14 as part of CVW-5, the squadron ventured into the NAG aboard *Kitty Hawk* in mid-February 2003. Whilst conducting combat missions alongside USAF assets in-theatre, VF-154 was asked by the latter to detach four aircraft and

The catapult crew give the all clear signal after checking that VF-213's 'Blacklion 105' is correctly attached to the launch shuttle aboard CVN-71 in early 2003. (US Navy)

'Blacklion 111' (BuNo 159629) of VF-213 is directed back to the fantail soon after recovering aboard CVN-71 after flying CVW-8's first OIF mission against targets near Falluja on 22/23 March 2003. The aircraft launched with three JDAM, two AIM-9s and a single AIM-54. Only the missiles returned with the jet to the carrier. (Troy Quigley)

four crews to provide dedicated FAC(A) and SCAR support for Coalition fast jets flying out of Al Udeid air base, in Qatar. Aside from performing these missions, the VF-154 Tomcat crews were also given the responsibility of instructing their F-15E brethren from the 336th FS/4th FW on how to conduct effective FAC(A) and SCAR.

According to VF-154's post-cruise summary of its contribution to OIF, 'Never in recent history had a carrier-based strike fighter squadron been tasked to fight a war from ashore and at sea at the same time. FAC(A) specialist crews on the beach amassed more than 300 combat hours and delivered more than 50,000 lbs of ordnance in 21 days of flying with their four crews and four jets.'

The unit did not escape from its shore-based foray unscathed, however, for on the night of 1 April the crew of a VF-154 jet was forced to eject over southern Iraq when its Tomcat suffered a single (port) engine and fuel transfer system failure. The transmission failure caused the remaining 'good' engine to run dry, so the crew were forced to 'bang out' over hostile territory – they were quickly retrieved by a Combat Search and Rescue team sent in from Kuwait.

The shore detachment returned to CV-63 in the second week of April, and by

the end of the aerial campaign on the 14th of the month, VF-154 had dropped 358 LGBs during 286 combat sorties.

The war waged by the two Mediter-ranean-based carriers contrasted markedly with that fought by the vessels sailing in the NAG. With Turkey having denied the US Army's 4th Infantry Division use of its territory as a jumping-off point, northern front activities centred on the support of SOF teams operating behind enemy lines. The teams relied heavily on close-air support

A section of VF-32 jets take up station off the left wing of a KC-135 prior to taking on fuel mid-way through their mission over Iraq in April 2003. Both jets appear to have expended a single LGB apiece, as only a solitary GBU-12 can be seen beneath each aircraft. The Tomcat nearest to the camera is BuNo 163224. The second jet is BuNo 161608. (USAF)

VF-32's 'Gypsy 114' (BuNo 161424) comes under tension on bow catapult two in early April 2003, the aircraft carrying two 2,000-lb JDAM. Flying 90 combat hours during the course of 21 sorties, the jet dropped four GBU-31s in OIF, as well as ten GBU-16s and twelve GBU-12s. (Erik Lenten)

This amazing photograph of a GBU-12 heading for its target (an SA-2 SAM site, some 20,000 ft below) was taken by a TARPS-equipped VF-32 jet during OIF. (VF-32)

(CAS) from CVW-3 and CVW-8, the latter embarked in CVN-71, which was also positioned in the eastern Mediterranean. F-14s from both air wings flew CAS missions in support of SOF units, often putting ordnance dangerously close to friendly forces. The sorties that these aircraft flew undoubtedly saved the lives of Coalition

forces on the ground, and eventually led to the capitulation of 100,000 Iraqi soldiers.

Prior to immersing itself in CAS missions with SOF, both VF-32 and VF-213 had completed a number of conventional strikes with JDAM and LGBs against fixed targets in Iraq. These missions, flown at the start of the conflict, were some of the longest of the war, covering distances of up to 800 miles each way. As the Tomcat had proven in OEF, it was more than capable of handling such sorties, and the mission lead for these more conventional strikes was often an F-14 crew. Further strikes on fixed targets followed, with mission times being reduced slightly once Turkey permitted overflights.

CVW-3 was designated as the day carrier throughout OIF, whilst CVW-8 handled much of the night work. VF-213 soon dubbed its nocturnal missions 'Vampire' sorties, with jets

◄ Both VF-32 and VF-213 regularly carried mixed weapon loads in OIF, this 'Blacklions' jet boasting a 500-lb GBU-12 LGB and a 2,000-lb GBU-31(V)2/B JDAM. (VF-213)

◄ Old meets new in May 2003 over Virginia; VF-2's CAG jet and one of the first two F/A-18F Super Hornets issued to newly redesignated VFA-2 when the 'Bounty Hunters' performed their fly-in to Oceana at the end of their OIF cruise. By month-end the last of the unit's F-14s had gone and VFA-2 had begun moving base from Oceana to Lemoore, in California. (VF-2)

regularly launching from the pitch-black deck of CVN-71 into poor weather conditions. The constant night operations eventually inspired the aircrew to coin the phrase 'living after midnight, bombing 'til the dawn'!

One of the more unusual missions flown by VF-213 saw the unit providing CAP for the airborne assault on Irbil air base, carried out by 1,000 paratroopers of the US Army's 173rd Airborne Brigade. Conducting the largest parachute drop since World War II, the soldiers jumped from a fleet of C-17s into Kurdish-controlled northern Iraq. The Globemasters were escorted by three waves of strike aircraft from CVN-71, with the US Navy jets also bombing Iraqi command and control bunkers and troop and artillery positions close to nearby Bashur airfield.

As the war progressed, CAS for SOF teams became the staple mission for both

VF-32 and VF-213, and their success in this role was related by the commander of CVW-8, Capt David Newland:

> Dropping precision-guided ordnance for a SOF team was a mission that gave immediate gratification. They were told where to aim the munitions, and they got direct feedback from the troops after they had expended their bombs.

By the time VF-213 ceased combat operations in OIF on 15 April, its crews had flown 198 combat sorties and 907.6 combat flight hours, with a 100 per cent sortie completion rate. 196 precision-guided munitions weighing 250,000 lbs had been expended, with 102 of these being LGBs and the remaining 94 JDAM. VF-32 completed 268 sorties and 1135.2

VF-213's 'Blacklion 213' circles in the low-holding pattern several miles astern of CVN-71 at the end of an OIF patrol in October 2005. This was the most colourful Tomcat in the unit during VF-213's final deployment with the Grumman fighter. It expended a solitary GBU-12, two GBU-38s and 500 rounds of 20 mm ammunition on 6-7 November 2005. (Lt Scott Timmester)

Its tanks topped off, VF-31's 'Tomcatter 107' drops away from a USAF KC-135 over Iraq and heads out on patrol. This aircraft flew 160 sorties during VF-31's 2005-06 deployment, after which it was retired to the Sabre Society's Hickory Aviation Museum. (USAF)

A sight to gladden the hearts of Tomcat proponents the world over. VF-31 and VF-213 get ready for a mass launch of 20 F-14Ds from CVN-71 off the Virginia coast to mark the end of the jet's final cruise on 10 March 2006. (US Navy)

hours in combat, dropping 247 LGBs and 118 JDAM (totalling 402,600 lbs). Its crews also expended 1,128 rounds of 20 mm high explosive incendiary in strafing passes.

The F-14 remained an important asset for the US Navy in its post-OIF I operations over Iraq, the aircraft supporting Coalition forces as they struggled to keep the rising insurgency in check. VF-211 (2003-04), VF-11 (2004), VF-143 (2004), VF-103 (2004) and VF-32

(2005) all completed their final cruises with the Tomcat during this period, performing missions similar to those flown during the invasion in 2003. By the autumn of 2005 just two Tomcat units remained in service with the US Navy, with all other fighter squadrons having by then re-equipped with the E- or F-model Super Hornet. Upon their transition to the new Boeing aircraft, the squadrons were re-designated as strike fighter units.

The Tomcat's final deployment commenced in September 2005 when F-14D-equipped VF-31 and VF-213 teamed up with CVW-8 aboard CVN-71. Both units would see considerable action over Iraq during the cruise, which lasted until early March 2006 – the final combat trap for the F-14 was made by a VF-213 jet on 8 February 2006. By the time the squadrons returned to Oceana, they had logged 1,163 sorties, 6,876 flight hours and dropped 9,500 lbs of ordnance in anger.

After 36 years of Fleet service, the Tomcat was officially retired on 22 September 2006. The last flight performed by a US Navy F-14 came on 4 October when VF-31's 'Tomcatter 101' made the short trip from Oceana to Farmingdale, New York, where it was subsequently placed on static display in front of the Northrop Grumman headquarters at nearby Bethpage.

'As a career F-14 pilot since 1992, I would be much happier flying the Tomcat until the end of my days in the Navy. But instead we have to enjoy this as long as we can. It's a Cold War icon with modern-day lethality. It represents all that our country used to battle, being designed to defend the fleet against "Bears" and "Badgers" flying over the Russian horizon. Now, it's morphed into the CAS machine of choice for current operations in Iraq. As our last combat cruise to the NAG clearly showed, the Tomcat is retiring at the top of its game. We're not wimping into the sunset. We're carrying a big stick right to the very end. The only sad thing is that I think we could have carried this big stick for a few more years yet.'

Cdr Jim Howe, Last commanding officer of VF-31
USS *Theodore Roosevelt* (CVN-71)

◄
Devoid of any VF-31 markings, 'Tomcatter 102' was supposed to perform the last official flight of an F-14 in US Navy service on 22 September 2006 at NAS Oceana. However, its port engine refused to light off, so the jet was taxied out of sight of the assembled crowd and the crew jumped into the strategically placed 'Tomcatter 107' – which, of course, proudly featured VF-31's 'Felix and the bomb' motif on its twin fins! (US Navy)

SPECIFICATIONS

F-14A Tomcat

Crew:	pilot and radar intercept officer
Length:	62 ft 8 in (19.10 m)
Wingspan:	64 ft 1.5 in (19.55 m) wings spread, 38 ft 2.4 in (11.65 m) wings at full sweep, and 33 ft 3.5 in (10.15 m) wings overswept for stowage
Wing Area:	565 sq ft (52.49 m²)
Height:	16 ft 0 in (4.88 m)
Weights:	39,921 lb (18,108 kg) empty and 74,349 lb (33,724 kg) maximum take-off weight
Service ceiling:	56,000 ft (17,070 m)
Maximum range:	1,740 nautical miles (3,220 km)
Maximum speed:	1,553 mph (2,485 kmh)
Cruising speed:	463-636 mph (741-1,019 kmh)
Engines:	two 20,900 lb st (93 kN) Pratt & Whitney TF30-P-414A afterburning turbofans
Armament:	one M61A1 Vulcan 20 mm cannon with 675 rounds of ammunition, up to eight air-to-air missiles (AIM-54A/C Phoenix, AIM-9L/M Sidewinder and AIM-7F/M Sparrow) on four wing glove and four fuselage stores pylons and up to 14,500 lb (6,577 kg) of conventional bombs

F-14B/D Tomcat

Crew:	pilot and radar intercept officer
Length:	62 ft 8 in (19.10 m)
Wingspan:	64 ft 1.5 in (19.55 m) wings spread, 38 ft 2.4 in (11.65 m) wings at full sweep, and 33 ft 3.5 in (10.15 m) wings overswept for stowage
Wing Area:	565 sq ft (52.49 m²)
Height:	16 ft 0 in (4.88 m)
Weights:	41,780 lb (18,950 kg) empty and 74,349 lb (33,724 kg) maximum take-off weight
Service ceiling:	53,000 ft (16,154 m)
Maximum range:	1,600 nautical miles (2,965 km)
Maximum speed:	1,248 mph (1,997 kmh)
Cruising speed:	477 mph (764 kmh)
Engines:	two 23,100 lb st (103 kN) General Electric F110-GE-400 afterburning turbofans
Armament:	one M61A1 Vulcan 20 mm cannon with 675 rounds of ammunition, up to eight air-to-air missiles (AIM-54A/C Phoenix, AIM-9L/M Sidewinder and AIM-7F/M Sparrow) on four wing glove and four fuselage stores pylons and up to 14,500 lb (6,577 kg) of conventional bombs

APPENDIX 2

MILESTONES

1968

21 June: Naval Air Systems Command issues a request for proposals for a two-man, supersonic, carrier-based aircraft incorporating variable-sweep wings. The project is designated VFX.

December: The Grumman F-111B, which was the end product of the controversial TFX programme, is cancelled after seven years of development.

1969

14 January: Grumman's Design 303 is selected as the winner of the VFX competition. The aircraft included the AN/AWG-9 radar, fire control system, AIM-54 Phoenix missile and Pratt & Whitney TF30 engines that had all been developed for the F-111B.

3 February: Grumman receives its first Tomcat contract from the US Navy.

1970

November: The first full scale development F-14A is rolled out by Grumman at its Long Island factory and subsequently commences taxi and pre-flight tests.

21 December: The F-14A completes its first flight from Grumman's airfield in Calverton. Nine days later it crashes due to hydraulic failure on only its second flight.

1971

24 May: Flight-testing resumes with the second full scale development F-14A.

27 May: The F-14B and F-14C are cancelled by Deputy Defense Secretary David Packard due to chronic budget overruns and ongoing technical problems with the Pratt & Whitney F401 engine.

2 September: The F-14A's variable-sweep wings are swept fully back in flight for the first time.

16 September: The aircraft makes its first supersonic flight.

2 December: Test pilot Cdr G W White becomes the first serving Naval Aviator to fly the F-14, nine of which have now been assigned to various test programmes.

1972

13 June: An F-14 is craned aboard USS *Forrestal* (CVA-59) at Pier 12 in the Norfolk navy yard. Two days later, with CVA-59 sailing off the Virginia coast, the aircraft becomes the first Tomcat to be launched from an aircraft carrier.

28 June: The Tomcat completes its initial carrier trials aboard CVA-59, having made three catapult launches, two arrested landings, 13 touch and goes and three intentional wave-off approaches.

July: Naval Aviators from the Pacific Missile Test Center become the first crew in military history to attack separate targets at the same time with multiple AIM-54As fired from a single fighter during F-14 tests at Point Mugu.

8 October: The first production-standard F-14A is delivered to fleet replacement squadron VF-124 at Miramar.

1973

1 July: VF-1 receives its first Tomcats, with VF-2 also getting a handful of F-14As during the month.

July: An F-14A crewed by Grumman test pilots participates in a fly-off at Andrews AFB for the benefit of the Shah of Iran and high-ranking IIAF officers.

21 November: During ongoing Phoenix missile tests, an F-14A fires six AIM-54As and guides them simultaneously towards six separate drone targets more than 50 miles away. Four direct hits are scored.

December: VF-14 and VF-32 commence their conversion to the F-14 from the F-4 with VF-124, these squadrons duly becoming the first East Coast Tomcat units upon their return to Oceana in July 1974.

1974

7 January: The first stage of the $2bn Project *Persian King* is signed between Iran, Grumman and Hughes.

May 1974: The first group of highly experienced IIAF F-4 pilots arrive at Miramar to begin their Tomcat instructor training with VF-124.

17 September: USS *Enterprise* (CVN-65) departs on a WestPac cruise with CVW-14 embarked. Included in the latter is VF-1 and VF-2, giving the Tomcat its operational debut.

1975

2 and 14 January: VF-1 loses two aircraft to engine failures whilst operating in the South China Sea.

29 April: F-14s from CVW-14 fly CAPs for US aircraft involved in Operation *Frequent Wind*, which sees all US personnel evacuated from South Vietnam.

28 June: VF-14 and VF-32 embark in USS *John F Kennedy* (CV-67) for the Tomcat's first Atlantic/ Mediterranean cruise.

5 December: The IIAF's first F-14A makes it maiden flight.

1976

24 January: The first two of 79 Tomcats eventually delivered to the IIAF arrive at newly built Khatami air base.

1980

7 September: An IRIAF F-14A from the 81st TFS gives the Tomcat its first aerial victory when its shoots down an IrAF Mi-25 attack helicopter with 20 mm cannon fire.

13 September: In the first aerial combat between 'swing wing' fighters, an IRIAF F-14A from the 81st TFS uses an AIM-54A missile to down an IrAF MiG-23MS. This is also the first time the Phoenix has been fired in anger.

1981

August: VF-84 gives TARPS its operational debut during the unit's Mediterranean cruise with CVW-8 aboard USS *Nimitz* (CVN-68).

19 August: Two LARAF Su-22s are shot down by a pair of F-14As from VF-41 embarked in CVN-68 after the US Navy jets are fired on by one of the 'Fitters' whilst exercising off the Libyan coast.

1983

25 October: VF-32 sends TARPS-equipped F-14As over Grenada in advance of the US invasion of the Caribbean island.

3 December: Two VF-31 aircraft performing a TARPS mission over Lebanon are fired on by Syrian SAM and AAA sites. The jets return to CV-67, and the following day these sites are targeted by carrier air strikes.

1985

10 October: Tomcats from VF-74 and VF-103, embarked in USS *Saratoga* (CV-60), are vectored onto an Egyptair Boeing 737 at night over the Mediterranean by an E-2C from VAW-125 and a USAF RC-135. The airliner, bound for Libya, has the terrorists who had recently hijacked the Italian cruise liner *Achille Lauro* on board. The Tomcat crews force the jet to land at NAS Sigonella, on Sicily, where the terrorists are apprehended by the Italian police.

1986

24-25 March: Aircraft from VF-74, VF-103, VF-33 and VF-102 provide escorts for US Navy strike aircraft attacking Libyan SAM sites that had fired on US jets flying over the Mediterranean.

14 April: Tomcats from the units listed in the previous entry provide fighter cover for USAFE F-111s sent to bomb targets in Libya from bases in the UK.

1987

26 March: An F-14A from VF-111 notches up the Tomcat's one millionth flight hour in US Navy service.

31 March: Grumman delivers the 557th, and last, production standard F-14A to the US Navy.

8 August: Two Tomcats from VF-21, embarked in USS *Constellation* (CV-64), intercept a pair of IRIAF F-4Es from the 91st TFW over the NAG, but fail to shoot the fighters down despite firing two Sparrow missiles at them.

16 November: The US Navy takes delivery of the first F-14A+ from Grumman, boasting the new, more powerful, F110 engines.

8 December: The F-14D prototype takes to the skies from Grumman's Calverton facility for the first time.

1988

18 April: F-14As from VF-213, embarked in USS *Enterprise* (CVN-65), warn off a formation of IRIAF F-4Es that attempt to intercept an E-2C during Operation *Praying Mantis*: a one-day war-at-sea against Iranian frigates that had been attacking supertankers in the NAG.

19 July: The first Gulf War comes to an end, by which time IRIAF F-14As have downed possibly as many as 159

IrAF aircraft. A further 34 claims remain unconfirmed. Up to 16 Tomcats have in turn been lost in almost eight years of bitter fighting.

1989
4 January: A pair of F-14As from VF-32, embarked in CV-67, shoot down two LARAF MiG-23s attempting to intercept them off the Libyan coast.

1990
8 March: VF-142 and VF-143, embarked in USS *Dwight D Eisenhower* (CVN-69), give the F-14A+ its operational debut during a routine Mediterranean deployment
23 March: The first production standard F-14D is rolled out at Grumman's Calverton plant
August: VF-21 and VF-154, embarked in USS *Independence* (CV-62), along with VF-142 and VF-143, protect Gulf states during Operation *Desert Shield* following Iraq's invasion of Kuwait.
8 August: The first live bombs dropped from a Fleet Tomcat are expended by an F-14B from VF-24 on targets near Yuma, Arizona.

18 October: VF-124 becomes the first Fleet squadron to receive the F-14D.

1991
17 January: Operation *Desert Storm* commences, as Coalition forces begin the job of ridding Kuwait of Iraqi forces. Some 99 Tomcats are part of the overwhelming air power brought to bear on the enemy.
21 January: An F-14A+ from VF-103 is shot down by a SAM during a TARPS mission. The pilot is rescued but the RIO becomes a PoW.
6 February: VF-1 becomes the only Tomcat unit to register an aerial victory in *Desert Storm* when one of its F-14As downs a Mi-8 helicopter with a Sidewinder missile.
1 May: All F-14A+s are redesignated F-14Bs.

1992
10 July: The US Navy accepts the final Tomcat built by Grumman. Some 679 examples had been delivered to the Fleet over the previous 22 years.

One of the most colourful Tomcats to serve with the US Navy, this F-14A was marked up as VX-4's 'Vandy One' for much of the 1980s. Having previously served with VF-124 and VF-213, it joined the 'Evaluators' at Point Mugu in 1979 and remained with the unit until retired in 1993. (US Navy)

1994

2 May: Two F-14Bs from VF-103, embarked in CV-60, achieve direct hits with three LGBs on a target range on the Italian island of Sardinia.

31 July: Lt Kara Hultgreen makes her first qualifying landing in an F-14A on board CV-64, and subsequently becomes the first female Tomcat pilot to join a Fleet squadron (VF-213). She is killed on 25 October, however, when her jet suffers engine failure whilst attempting to land aboard USS *Abraham Lincoln* (CVN-72).

1995

March: An F-14B test aircraft supplied by VF-103 drops and self-guides LGBs with the aid of LANTIRN for the first time.

5 September: Two F-14As from VF-41, embarked in CVN-68, drop LGBs (designated by F/A-18s) on an ammunition dump in eastern Bosnia during Operation *Allied Force*.

1996

14 June: The LANTIRN targeting system is officially introduced to the Fleet at Oceana. LANTIRN-equipped F-14Bs from VF-103 deploy with CVN-65 for the first time later that month and duly see operational service over Bosnia.

1998

16 December: F-14Bs from VF-32, embarked in USS *Harry S Truman* (CVN-75), spearhead Operation *Desert Fox*, which sees a wave of attacks against Iraqi air defence installations. Two days later, the F-14Ds of VF-213, operating from USS *Carl Vinson* (CVN-70), join in the action. During the four days of *Desert Fox*, VF-32 drops 111,054 lbs of LGBs.

1999

5 January: Two F-14Ds from VF-213 fire two AIM-54Cs at IrAF MiG-25s that penetrate the No-Fly Zone. Neither missile hits its target, however.

March–June: VF-14 and VF-41, flying from USS *Theodore Roosevelt* (CVN-71), are committed to Operation *Deliberate Force*, NATO's campaign to free Kosovo from

Serbian control. The units expend close to 800,000 lbs of LGBs and iron bombs during the campaign.

9 September: F-14Ds of VF-2, embarked in CV-64, play a leading part in the success of Operation *Gun Smoke*, a one-day bombing campaign against Iraqi SAM, AAA and radar sites. Aside from dropping LGBs, the unit also fire a single AIM-54C at an IrAF MiG-23, but it misses.

2001

11 September: VF-11 and VF-143 help defend the eastern seaboard from the deck of CV-67 in the immediate aftermath of the terrorist attacks on New York City and Washington, DC.

8 October: VF-14 and VF-41, embarked in CVN-65, and VF-213, operating from CVN-70, spearhead the first manned strikes on al-Qaeda and Taleban targets in Afghanistan as Operation *Enduring Freedom* commences. Jets from all three units rely heavily on the Tomcat's legendary endurance to reach the land-locked country, and the LANTIRN pod to allow them to employ LGBs.

23 October: VF-102, embarked in CVN-71, relieves VF-14 and VF-41 in OEF. Along with the rest of CVW-1, the unit subsequently spends a record-breaking 159 days at sea without a port call.

15 December: VF-211, operating from USS *John C Stennis* (CVN-74), relieves VF-213 in OEF.

2002

11 March: VF-11, flying F-14Bs from CV-67 in OEF, becomes the first unit to drop a JDAM in anger whilst supporting US forces participating in Operation *Anaconda*.

2003

21-22 March: VF-2, embarked in CV-64, is at the forefront of the 'Shock and Awe' strikes on Baghdad that signal the start of Operation *Iraqi Freedom*. Five squadrons operating 52 Tomcats from three carriers in the NAG and two in the eastern Mediterranean play an important part in removing Saddam Hussein from power.

1 April: One of four F-14As from VF-154 based ashore at Al Udeid, in Qatar, crashes in southern Iraq after suffering engine and fuel transfer system failure. This proves to be the only Tomcat lost in OIF, and its crew are quickly rescued.

28 August: VF-211, embarked in CVN-65, departs Norfolk on the F-14A's final operational deployment, which ends on 29 February 2004.

2004

24 May: VF-31, equipped with the F-14D, joins CVN-74 at the start of the final WestPac for the Tomcat. The deployment ends on 1 November.

13 October: VF-32, embarked in CVN-75, starts the final deployment for the F-14B. Subsequently seeing combat over Iraq, the unit finally returns to Oceana on 18 April 2005.

2005

1 September: CVW-8, with F-14D-equipped VF-31 and VF-213 assigned, embarks in CVN-71 and departs for the Mediterranean and the NAG. This will be the final cruise for the Tomcat.

11 October: Whilst on a patrol over Iraq, a VF-213 jet drops the first ordnance to be expended by CVW-8 in anger on cruise.

2006

8 February: F-14Ds from VF-31 and VF-213 launch from CVN-71 on the Tomcat's final combat mission. A jet from VF-31 drops a bomb during the sortie, and a VF-213 jet records the last combat carrier trap for the F-14.

10 March: VF-31 and VF-213 fly in to Oceana at the end of the Tomcat's final combat deployment. By the time the squadrons had returned home, they had logged 1,163 sorties, 6,876 flight hours and dropped 9,500 lbs of ordnance in anger.

28 July: A VF-31 jet makes the final carrier launch for the F-14, being catapulted from the deck of CVN-71 as the vessel sails off the coast of Virginia.

22 September: After 36 years of Fleet service, the Tomcat is officially retired by the US Navy at Oceana.

An F-14D from VF-213 heads north into Iraq at sunset on 23 October 2006. (Lt Scott Timmester)

4 October: VF-31's 'Tomcatter 101' performs the last flight by a US Navy F-14 when its makes the short trip from Oceana to Farmingdale, New York, where it is subsequently placed on static display in front of the Northrop Grumman headquarters at nearby Bethpage.

A sad end to a once mighty warrior. This ex-Naval Air Warfare Center F-14A was unceremoniously devoured by a Caterpillar 330C mechanical excavator at Davis-Monthan AFB. Following a directive from the Department of Defense, AMARG instigated an accelerated scrapping programme for the F-14 in 2007 in an effort to prevent Iran from securing valuable spare parts for its Tomcat fleet. (USAF)